Toproping

Bob Gaines

FALCONGUIDES

GUILFORD, CONNECTICUT
HELENA, MONTANA
AN IMPRINT OF GLOBE PEQUOT PRESS

FALCONGUIDES®

FalconGuides is an imprint of Globe Pequot Press.
Falcon, FalconGuides, and Outfit Your Mind are registered trademarks of Morris Book Publishing, LLC.

Project editor: David Legere
Text design and layout: Casey Shain

Photos by Bob Gaines unless otherwise noted. Photo, page viii–ix, © Tom Grundy, licensed by Shutterstock.com

Library of Congress Cataloging-in-Publication data is on file.

ISBN 978-0-7627-7032-8

Printed in the United States of America

10 9 8 7 6 5 4 3 2 1

Contents

Chapter 7: Belaying from the Top

Chapter 8: Advanced Toprope Anchor Rigging Systems

Chapter 9: Basic Assistance and Rescue Skills

Chapter 10: Teaching Rock Climbing in a Toprope Environment

Chapter 11: Risk Management

Chapter 12: Leave No Trace Ethics

Acknowledgments

First of all I'd like to thank John Burbidge at FalconGuides for putting it all together.

Thanks to the climbers who posed for photos: Michael Bains, Patty Kline, Steve Schwartz, Nicole Miyoshi, and Vivian Koo.

Thanks to the guides who posed while demonstrating techniques: Tony Sartin, Terri Condon, Tony Grice, Ryan Murphy, Reggie Bulman, Kevin Jackson, Bryan Baez, Robin Depke, Ryan Bennet, William Jaques, and Adam Radford.

Thanks also to my fellow guides and mentors, from whom I've learned a great deal: Adam Fox, Jon Tierney, Alan Jolley, Peter Croft, Scott Cosgrove, Marcus Jollif, Todd Vogel, Erik Kramer-Webb, Tony Grice, Tony Sartin, Pat Dennis, and Dave Mayville.

Special thanks to John Long for the many insightful conversations we had while working on the *Climbing Anchors* books.

Thanks to my wife, Yvonne, for her help with the photography, and for being my number one climbing partner.

Introduction

Toproping is the safest way to practice rock climbing techniques. For many enthusiasts it is the most enjoyable form of rock climbing. It's true that bouldering, with its inherent simplicity, is less complicated than toproping, with a great sense of freedom of movement, unfettered by complicated gear and rigging—the only equipment needed is your shoes, chalk bag, and maybe a crash pad with a buddy to spot you while you push your limits in a relatively safe environment. But bouldering is very limiting in another way: The higher you climb above the ground, the scarier it gets. And one thing is certain: When you fall, you hit the ground. Hitting the crash pad from 10 feet off the ground can be a bone-jarring experience. Many of my fellow climbers sustained the most serious injuries of their entire climbing careers because of a fall while bouldering.

Lead climbing is both physically and mentally challenging—figuring out not only the moves, but also the complexities of protection placements along the way. The mental focus required to lead difficult trad (traditional) routes is intense, including the psychological aspect that comes into play when you move high above your protection, risking a long leader fall. Sport climbing is less demanding psychologically, allowing you to push physical boundaries, but stopping and clipping a long series of bolts interrupts the purity of the flow.

Free soloing has been said to be the purest form of rock climbing, but there is a fine line between the pure joy of fun-in-the-sun rock climbing, moving and flowing up the climb with nothing but air beneath your feet, and the sudden shadow of fear that can take over as quickly as a dark cloud eclipsing the sun. The free soloist faces the possibility of the ultimate irony: falling and dying as a direct result of being afraid to die, knowingly risking life for the pleasure of pure, unfettered freedom of movement.

So for many, toproping is the most relaxing form of rock climbing, and definitely the safest. With the practice of sound safety fundamentals, the toprope climber, free from the psychological fear of falling, uninterrupted from any need to place or clip protection, can achieve a zen-like purity of focused movement rarely attained in the other forms of rock climbing. For the novice, toproping is the best and safest way to practice technique—unlike bouldering, where falls can be sudden and off-balance because knowing when a fall is imminent has not yet become instinctive. Once you learn the fundamentals of knots, anchoring, and belaying, toprope climbing is the best and safest method to quickly hone technique without the risk of potentially injurious falls.

This book is written from an instructor's perspective. For over twenty-five years I've worked as a professional climbing guide and manager of a rock climbing school working in a toprope environment. Many of the techniques in this book were learned over these years. From every guide I've worked with along the way, I've gleaned some modicum of knowledge. In recent years I've received training from some of the top mentors in the country through the American Mountain Guides Association, discussing techniques for teaching rock climbing in a toprope setting and staying current with state-of-the-art methods. I'm currently an instructor for the AMGA's Single Pitch Instructor Course,

and many of the principals in this book are a result of my exposure to and collaboration with other instructors.

For the beginner, this book will give you all the information you need to get started. For the intermediate climber, this book will be helpful to refresh your knowledge on key concepts and to learn some new ones. For the experienced climber, this book will reinforce fundamentals and give you some new methods for rigging topropes.

Whether you are taking a few friends or family members out climbing, or teaching a group of clients as a professional, the responsibility of a safe outing is in your hands. The fundamentals of safe rigging and risk management are the same whether or not you are a professional. My goal in this book is to pass along some of the things I've learned from experience: what to watch out for, and how to streamline the rigging of safe toprope anchor systems.

This book is designed to be used in conjunction with the other books in FalconGuide's How To Climb series, namely *How to Rock Climb,* 5th edition, by John Long, and *Climbing Anchors* (along with the *Climbing Anchors Field Guide*), by John Long and myself. If you have not already read these books, I encourage you to do so to strengthen your foundation of knowledge.

Toproping is the safest way to practice technique and build confidence.

Getting Started

Site Selection

The ideal toprope crag is less than 100 feet high, with an aesthetic, sheer face of rock. It offers an easy walk to the top of the cliff; bomber anchors; clean, solid rock that minimizes rockfall danger; and a flat, comfortable base for belaying and hanging out. The perfect cliff has numerous routes at the level you find enjoyable and challenging for a fun day at the crag. To find your ideal crag, consult a climbing guidebook or ask for recommendations at your local climbing retail shop.

Guidebooks and Ratings

Guidebooks will usually give you a description of how difficult it is to approach and descend from a particular cliff, along with a description of the location and rating of the routes on the cliff. Most guidebooks include topos—either a photo of the cliff with the route lines marked, along with a verbal description; or a diagram of the routes, with the route lines marked and symbols identifying the location of features like cracks, corners, chimneys, trees, bolts, fixed rappel anchors, etc. Studying a

Above, A topo is a photo or other diagram detailing the location of the routes on a particular cliff.

Students getting their start during a basic rock climbing class at Joshua Tree National Park.

guidebook's description can tell you if the top of a particular cliff can be easily approached and descended without any Class 4 or 5 climbing. Well-known toproping cliffs are usually popular because they have easy access, good anchors, and good-quality climbs.

This is the Class 1–5 rating system:

Class 1: Walking on relatively flat ground and trail hiking

Class 2: Hiking over rough ground, such as scree and talus; may include the use of hands for stability

Class 3: Scrambling that requires the use of hands and careful foot placement

A Typical Day of Toproping

John and Jill had done their homework and studied the guidebook before they arrived at their crag of choice. From the parking area it was just a short hike to the crag. It was a fine spring day, sunny but cool, and as luck would have it, they had the crag all to themselves. Jill pulled the guidebook out of her pack and surveyed the rock face.

"It says the approach to the top is Class 3 over on the north side. Let's gear up here. There are a bunch of routes we can set up!"

They put on their harnesses and sorted their rack. Between them they had two sets of cams to 3 inches, plus a good selection of nuts, carabiners, and slings, two cordelettes, a 100-foot low-stretch rigging rope, and a 60-meter dynamic climbing rope. They both were wearing approach shoes with sticky rubber, which gave them confidence in their footing for the short but exposed scramble to the top.

"Let's set up the 5.6 to warm up," John said.

They built two separate anchors—each with three cams equalized with a cordelette—and then used their extension rope, configured in the Joshua Tree System, to extend the rigging over the edge of the cliff so that the climbing rope would not be running over a sharp edge that could cause wear or even cut it. They each used a prusik on one leg of the rigging rope, which was connected to a sling attached to their harness, to protect themselves as they approached the edge. They each rappelled down by pre-rigging their ATC rappel devices onto the climbing rope, backed up with an autoblock knot.

When they were both back down at the base, Jill built a ground anchor by slinging a tunnel between two boulders. Since John outweighed her by a hundred pounds, she'd learned to always anchor herself when belaying him so she wouldn't get pulled from her stance if he fell. She tied into the end of the rope and connected herself to the ground anchor with a clove hitch, a knot that allowed her to easily adjust the length of the anchor rope. They checked each other's harness buckles and knots, a safety ritual they always went through before every climb.

"On belay?" John asked.

"Belay on," Jill responded.

"Climbing," John said.

"Climb on," Jill responded. These well-practiced commands were standard on all their climbs and allowed them to make absolutely certain that each knew what the other person was doing.

Class 4: Scrambling over steep and exposed terrain; a rope may be used for safety on exposed areas

Class 5: Technical "free" climbing where terrain is steep and exposed, requiring the use of ropes, protection hardware, and related techniques; *see Yosemite Decimal System (YDS)*

Class 6: Aid climbing where climbing equipment is used for balance, rest, or progress; denoted with a capital A followed by numerals 0 to 5 (e.g., 5.9/A3 means the free climbing difficulties are up to 5.9 with an aid section of A3 difficulty)

Jill belayed John while he did the climb. When he reached the top and was ready to be lowered, John yelled, "Tension."

"Tension on," Jill said as she pulled the rope tight to hold John's weight.

"Lower me," John said.

"Lowering," Jill said, and she slowly began to feed rope through her belay device while John "walked" down the climb in a sitting position with his feet out in front of him.

When he got to the ground, John said, "Off belay."

"Belay off," Jill said. She took the rope out of her belay device, untied from the ground anchor, and got ready to climb.

They both did the climb twice, and when Jill reached the top the second time, she topped-out to rig another climb. "Off belay," she called to John, after she was safe. "Belay off" was John's response, after he had unclipped the rope from his belay device.

Jill rigged another anchor on the highest part of the cliff directly above the next climb they wanted to toprope, a steep and intimidating 5.8 crack. Her anchor consisted of four cams in two separate cracks, equalized to a master point with slings and a cordelette. From the anchor to the edge of the cliff was a good 30 feet, down a severely sloping and exposed slab. To rig the extension rope, Jill decided to rig a self-belay using a Grigri on a tether. After she rigged her toprope using the Fox System, she rappelled down on her tether and then transitioned to a pre-rigged rappel on the doubled climbing rope. She backed up her rappel device with an autoblock. She had John tie knots in the ends of her rappel rope to close the system, a habit they always used while rappelling or toproping in a single-pitch scenario.

Jill knew the climb would be right at John's limit of difficulty (crack climbs were not his forte), so she placed a cam for a ground anchor and belayed him with the Grigri, anticipating that he might need to hang and rest. Sure enough, halfway up the crack John's forearms were pumped and he was struggling.

"Tension!" he yelled.

"Tension on," Jill responded, and since she was belaying with the Grigri and was tight to her ground anchor, it was easy to hold his weight. "I've got you," she said. "Take your time and rest up, it's no problem to hold you." After he hung for a few minutes, John said he was ready to climb again.

"You can do it!" Jill encouraged. John finished the climb and lowered down, a bit discouraged.

Jill waltzed up the crack, looking fairly relaxed. "You made it look easy," John said.

"Easy on a toprope," was Jill's response. "I don't know if I could lead that. Stopping to place protection would

Continued on next page

The Yosemite Decimal System

If you travel to foreign countries to go rock climbing, you'll notice that every country seems to have its own rating system, which can be a bit confusing. In American rock climbing we use what is known as the Yosemite Decimal System (YDS), which rates Class 5 climbs based on the most difficult section of the climb, called the crux, on a scale from 5.0 to 5.15. A climb graded 5.0 to 5.5 is usually appropriate for beginners, whereas a climb rated from 5.6 to 5.9 is considered intermediate level, and a climb graded 5.10 and higher is in the realm of experts and experienced climbers. The "rating" of a climb is such an abstract concept that to get a sense of what it really means, you need to get on the rock and experience a wide variety of techniques. For example, a low-angle slab that is as smooth as a pane of

Continued from previous page
take a lot more energy."

They took a break for lunch and scoped out some impressive face climbs on the right side of the cliff. "From the bolt anchor we can toprope the 5.9 and the 5.10a off the same anchor if we use a directional," John said.

"Great idea," said Jill. "A two for one deal!"

John climbed the crack again, this time without falling or hanging on the rope, a small victory for him. At the top, before going off belay, he clipped the tether into his Grigri and pulled the rope through it for protection as he ascended the 30-foot slab above the toprope rig's carabiners, up to the high master point of the anchor Jill had rigged. After he was safely above the exposed section, he yelled, "Off belay, Jill!" and de-rigged the anchor.

He walked over to the two-bolt anchor and decided to rig it using a cordelette and a self-equalizing "quad" rig, knowing that the direction of pull would change for each of the two climbs and the quad is a perfect anchor rig for that situation. One climb was directly below the anchor, and the other one started about 15 feet to the right. That climb would require a "directional," meaning the rope would have to run through a piece of protection to keep it above the climb and prevent the climber from swinging if a fall occurred. John tied stopper knots in both ends of the rope before tossing it down—the climb was nearly 100 feet high (half his rope length), and the side directional would make the rope even shorter. He rigged an autoblock backup for his rappel, allowing him to go hands-free as he set the directional anchor (two cams equalized with a sliding X) in a crack about 20 feet down and 15 feet right of his quad anchor.

Jill and John climbed both routes twice. When Jill reached the anchor the final time, she decided to rappel down because the two-bolt anchor was equipped with metal rings and the downclimb looked a little tricky. Before she went off belay, she took a sling, girth-hitched it to her harness, and clipped into one of the bolts with a locking carabiner as a safety. After telling John she was off belay, she threaded the rope through both rings, tying a stopper knot on the end she just untied from, and checked to make sure John left a knot in the other end. Then she rapped down to the base. Once on the ground she made sure the stopper knot was untied from one end of the rope before pulling down on the other end to retrieve the rope. She warned John when the end was almost through the anchor: "Heads up, John, rope coming down . . . ROPE!" so that John could move out of the way and not get whipped by the rope end. Jill coiled the rope and John reracked the gear. They packed up and made the short hike back to the parking area. At the car Jill pulled out a couple of cold drinks from a small cooler and handed one to John. "Here's to a great day of toproping," she said. "Cheers!"

Sticky rubber–soled approach shoes are indispensable for Class 2 and 3 terrain typically encountered while hiking to and from the crag.

glass can be rated the same as a big overhang with doorknob-size handholds.

The YDS was actually first developed in the 1950s at Tahquitz Rock, a 1,000-foot-high dome of granite that rises from a mountainside high above the town of Idyllwild, in Southern California. In the 1940s and '50s, local climbers often climbed their favorite Class 5 routes over and over again, rating them easy, moderate, or difficult Class 5. Eventually, when more routes were developed at Tahquitz, the climbers subdivided them into a scale of difficulty from 5.0 to 5.9. In 1952 Royal Robbins climbed the first 5.9 route in America when he made the first free ascent (i.e., without resorting to hanging on gear for aid or rest) of Tahquitz Rock's *Open Book* route. It wasn't until the 1960s that the first 5.10 routes were climbed in America, at Yosemite. It was here in Yosemite Valley that the YDS rating system was refined, and eventually the 5.11 and 5.12 grades were added. Today the most difficult climbs in the world are rated 5.15, and it's only a matter of time before someone climbs a 5.16.

One refinement of the YDS is that above 5.9 the grades are even further subdivided into four letter grades: a, b, c, and d, starting with 5.10a. For example, a 5.10d is the most difficult 5.10, and a 5.11a is the easiest 5.11.

Ratings are subjective, abstract concepts, and will seem right or wrong depending on your height, skill level, and other factors like temperature, the condition of your climbing shoes, and how much you drank the night before. The rating of a particular route is assigned by the first ascent party, who also gets the honor of naming the route. A "sandbag" rating is an underrated climb, done so usually for egotistical reasons. With today's social media, climbing websites often allow for everyone's opinion on a climb's rating, so the process has become more democratic, and guidebook authors will often change the rating of a climb due to general consensus.

The Big Picture

To understand where toproping fits into the grand scheme of things, you should understand the various types of climbing situations. Use the glossary in the back of this book to look up any undefined terms referenced in the text, as many of the techniques used in other types of climbing, like leading and multipitch climbing, are not covered in depth in this book. But to get things started, here's a breakdown of the main categories and subcategories of rock climbing.

Perhaps the simplest form of rock climbing is **bouldering**—climbing small rock faces and boulders without the use of any equipment other than climbing shoes and a chalk bag. A fall while bouldering guarantees you'll hit the ground, so many practitioners use a crash pad specifically designed for bouldering, along with a partner or two to spot them and help them land safely. The role of a spotter is not to physically catch a falling climber but to assist him, like in gymnastics, directing him with outstretched arms to help him land (hopefully) on his feet and in balance.

Toproping is climbing with the use of a top belay, typically on a cliff less than 100 feet high, with the rope running through a toprope anchor rigged at the top of the cliff. The climber is tied into one end of the rope, which goes up through the anchor and back down to the belayer. As the climber ascends the route, the belayer manages the slack, and is ready to hold the weight of the climber if he should fall. When the climber reaches the anchor, he is typically lowered back down to the ground by the belayer. Another toprope scenario is when the belayer belays from the top of the cliff as the climber ascends from below.

Leading is when a climber ties in to the end of the rope and climbs up the cliff, trailing the rope below her, with the belayer paying out rope as the leader climbs. The leader places **protection** (or pro) and clips the rope into the gear as she proceeds. If the leader falls (and the protection holds), she will fall at least twice the distance above the last piece of protection before the belayer can stop the fall. This is known as a **leader fall.** Once the climber reaches the end of the pitch (which can be only as long as the rope), she stops and builds a belay anchor, usually at a good ledge or stance. The second, or follower, cleans the gear as he climbs the pitch and reaches the belay anchor. If this is the top of the climb, it is called a one-pitch climb. A **pitch** is the distance between belay points. If the team proceeds higher, up another pitch, the climb becomes a multipitch climb. Big wall climbs in Yosemite, like those on El Capitan, have as many as thirty pitches.

Trad, or **traditional, climbing** is when gear (nuts, cams, etc.) is used for protection and anchors. Trad climbing can have some bolts thrown in the mix of protection and anchors, but involves mostly gear placements. **Sport climbing,** by definition, is an entirely bolted climb. No gear other than quickdraws (a short sling with two carabiners attached for clipping bolts), a few slings, and carabiners is required, as the protection consists entirely of bolts, usually spaced no more than a body length or two, and the anchor is a bolted anchor.

Free climbing is climbing the rock with a rope for protection, but not hanging on the rope or the equipment for assistance on the actual ascent. **Aid climbing** is a form of ascent that uses gear to support the climber's weight and make upward progress. **Free soloing** is climbing without a rope.

CHAPTER TWO

Basic Equipment

Harness

I began climbing before the advent of the modern climbing harness. Instead of a harness, I used a swami belt. I took a 20-foot length of 2-inch-wide nylon webbing (rated at 8,000 lb.), wrapped it a bunch of times around my waist, and tied it with a water knot. Then I tied my climbing rope around the swami belt with a figure eight follow-through. This setup discouraged **hangdogging** and was rib jarring in a leader fall! Soon we figured out how to add leg loops, which made the rig more comfortable to say the least!

Harnesses have come a long way since the swami belt days. Look for a model that has a belay loop and gear loops. If you'll be climbing in different seasons, with differing clothing, a harness with adjustable leg loops is a good choice. Top brands include Arc'teryx, Black Diamond, Petzl, Metolius, Wild Country, Singing Rock, Trango, Mammut, and Camp USA. Some newer models have webbing with "speed buckles" that are pre-threaded and already doubled back, so all you have to do is loosen them before you put the harness on, then tighten the webbing to fit. Some harnesses have the old-school "double pass" buckle, where the webbing belt must be doubled back through the buckle. Check the manufacturer's guidelines on the harness

Modern, lightweight climbing harness.

Basic equipment for toproping includes nuts, camming devices, carabiners, slings, and cordelettes.

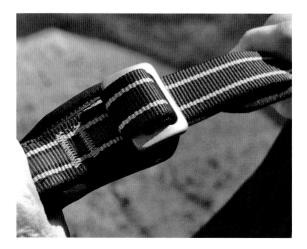

Traditional, doubled-back buckle.

Modern "speed buckle."

you buy and read the instructions on how to properly buckle and use the harness.

You'll want to retire your harness if the belay loop becomes frayed or shows signs of wear. Petzl recommends using nylon products no longer than seven years, even with minimal use.

Shoes

In the 1970s the EB was the best rock climbing shoe. The rubber wasn't very sticky, so most of the difficult routes during that era were done with precise and exacting edging technique. Around 1980 the first sticky rubber shoe of the modern era, called the FIRE (pronounced FEE-ray), was sold by Boreal, and it revolutionized face climbing. Now most of the extreme slab routes can be done via smearing technique, and the extreme face climbs of the 1970s seem significantly easier. I can remember the first time I wore FIREs, testing them out on the Camp 4 boulders in Yosemite. I was able to do many boulder problems I could never touch before, thanks to the magical smearing ability of the new rubber.

A myriad of styles and models of climbing shoes are on the market today, all with very sticky rubber.

Harness with adjustable leg loops.

Selection of rock climbing shoes at Nomad Ventures climbing shop in Idyllwild, California.

There will always be debate over which brand of rubber is the stickiest, but the gold standard for many years has been the Five Ten brand's "C4" rubber. If you ask a climbing shoe resoler which rubber is the most requested for use as a resole, no doubt the answer will be Five Ten C4.

For your first climbing shoe, choose a shoe that you feel fits your foot the best and is comfortable. After you become obsessed with rock climbing, you'll probably own several shoes for different types of climbing. Top climbing shoe brands include Five Ten, La Sportiva, Mad Rock, Evolve, and Scarpa.

Chalk Bag

Once you start using chalk, you'll no doubt become hopelessly addicted (like I am). There is no question chalk will help provide a better grip, particularly on

A chalk bag should have a belt so you can move it around your waist and a drawstring closure to keep the chalk from spilling out when you're not using it. Chalk is sold in small blocks that can be crushed into powder.

more difficult routes in warmer conditions. I like to use a chalk bag on a belt so that I can move it from side to side, or away from my back when I'm climbing wide cracks or chimneys. The Endo brand, distributed by Frank Endo, has always been my favorite. A soft brush (like a toothbrush) is useful for brushing away excess chalk and cleaning dirt off holds.

Helmets

Back in the 1960s and '70s, very few climbers (less than 10 percent, I'd say) wore helmets. You were considered a geek and "not cool" if you wore a helmet. Today it's the opposite. Most climbers (probably around 80 percent) wear helmets, particularly in trad climbing areas.

Even in the seemingly benign toprope environment, hazards do exist. Rockfall can be a threat, especially if there is loose rock at the top of the cliff. Be especially aware when other climbers are at the top, rigging anchors and setting ropes, as rocks are easily dislodged by ropes being pulled around. When teaching groups, I always establish a mandatory helmet zone at the base of the cliff, and then watch for clients who are lounging at the base without a helmet.

If you are on the cliff or at the top of the cliff and dislodge a rock (or any object), the universal signal is "ROCK!" How loud the signal is yelled usually signifies the size of the rock. My closest calls in over thirty years of climbing have been with near-miss rockfalls. If the warning comes from 100 feet or more away, you may want to look up, judge the trajectory, and move aside accordingly. If the signal comes from just above you, and you haven't seen it happen, you might just want to hunker down and not look up, so as not to get hit in the face. Obviously, wearing a helmet is a good idea when climbing, belaying from the base of the climb, and hanging out at the bottom of the cliff.

Whether or not you choose to wear a helmet is up to you, but be aware that many fatal climbing

A selection of modern climbing helmets from Nomad Ventures climbing shop, Joshua Tree, California.

incidents could have been prevented if the climber was wearing a helmet. Rockfall, whether caused by other climbers, the rope, or natural causes, is always a danger. Top brands of climbing helmets include Petzl, Black Diamond, Mammut, and Camp USA.

Rope

There are three basic types of ropes used in climbing: dynamic, low-stretch, and static. A dynamic rope is the most commonly used rope for toproping and lead climbing; it will stretch up to 20 to 30 percent during a leader fall and around 10 percent in a toprope fall. A low-stretch rope has relatively low stretch, and therefore should not be used for lead climbing, because rope stretch is the key to absorbing the energy generated in a leader fall. A static rope, by definition, is just that—very low stretch. Think of it like a wire cable. Static ropes generally have very poor handling characteristics due to their stiffness and are typically used for fixed lines, hauling, and rappelling, where dynamic properties are not required.

Rope stretch is one of the hazards inherent in a toprope situation. Modern dynamic ropes stretch approximately 8 or 9 percent under body weight. Picture a 100-foot-high cliff set up as a toprope,

using a dynamic rope. At the start of the climb, you'll have 200 feet of rope in the system.

Let's say you're belaying a climber, with a bit of slack, who falls 15 feet up the route. Do the math: 180 feet times 8 percent equals 14.4 feet. Chances are your climber will hit the ground, as there is even more stretch from the additional force created by even a small amount of slack. (In a severe leader fall, the rope will stretch 25 to 35 percent.)

In my climbing school program we've used low-stretch ropes (also called low-elongation or semi-static ropes) for our toproping classes for more than twenty-five years. These ropes stretch about 3 to 4 percent under body weight, slightly more in a toprope fall with a bit of slack. From a risk management standpoint, it just makes sense to use a low-stretch rope for toprope situations, especially if you're setting up relatively long routes (up to 100 feet high). The characteristics I look for in a low-stretch rope are EN 1891 certification, Type A designation, elongation in the 3 to 4 percent range under body weight, and a suppleness that tells you the rope will hold knots firmly and handle well for belaying. Sterling makes an excellent low-stretch rope called the Safety Pro. I prefer the 10.5 mm diameter for good handling and durability.

Selection of ropes at Nomad Ventures climbing shop, Idyllwild, California.

With technological advancements in rope manufacturing, modern "static" ropes stretch hardly at all, some as little as 1% under body weight. These ropes should not be used for toprope belaying, but can be used for anchor rigging, although I also prefer a low-stretch for that application.

If using a dynamic rope for toprope belaying, beware of the dangers of rope stretch, and keep the rope taut in situations where the climber is just off the ground, or just above a ledge.

A good choice for your first rope is a 60-meter by 10.5 mm-diameter rope. You'll have a choice of a "dry coating" versus a "non-dry" rope. The dry coating is applied so the rope will not absorb water,

which is useful for alpine climbing and mountaineering and climbing in wet conditions, as a wet rope is weaker. For pure rock climbing in dry conditions, save your money and buy a non-dry rope; the dry coating wears off after only a few days of toproping anyway.

Recently there has been a trend toward ever-thinner ropes. Ropes as thin as 9.2 mm in diameter are UIAA rated for lead climbing. But these thinner ropes are stretchier and will wear out far more quickly. For toproping I don't recommend going below 10 mm in diameter for your climbing rope, and 10.5 mm will be more durable in the long run.

Rope Care and Use

When buying a climbing rope, purchase it from a climbing shop that specializes in selling climbing gear. A dynamic climbing rope should have UIAA (Union Internationale des Associations d'Alpinisme) and/or CE (Certified for Europe) certification to EN (European Norm) 892. This means the rope has been tested and approved by a UIAA-approved testing facility. Static and low-stretch (or low-elongation) ropes are tested in Europe to meet EN 1891. In the United States, static and low-stretch ropes are tested by UL (Underwriters Laboratories) to meet NFPA 1983 (National Fire Protection Association Standard). Any reputable climbing shop will only stock the top brands, like Sterling, Maxim, Beal, Bluewater, Mammut, Edelrid, Edelweiss, Petzl, Millet, Metolius, and PMI.

Avoid setting up a toprope where your rope might abrade over an edge when someone is being lowered. This can severely weaken or ruin your sheath in just one climb/lower cycle! Avoid standing or stepping on your rope, as this can grind sharp pebbles and grit through the sheath and into the core. A tarp or rope bag is useful in areas where the base of the cliff is sandy or dirty. This will keep your rope neater and cleaner and prevent it from picking up silt and dirt that can wear out your carabiners and belay device faster. Minimize your rope's exposure to UV light, as this will weaken the fibers over time. Store your rope in a shaded, dry place.

If your rope gets dirty, you can wash it by hand in a tub, or in a washing machine (preferably a front-loading washing machine, because a top-loading machine's agitator will abrade the rope) with hot water and soap suitable for nylon. If washing your rope in a bathtub, make sure the tub is free from any chemicals that may damage it. I daisy chain the full length of my rope before washing it in a machine to keep it from getting tangled. Let your rope dry by hanging it in a shaded area.

Be vigilant and protect your rope from coming into contact with any chemicals that contain acids, bleaching or oxidizing agents, and alkalines. Acid is the arch enemy of nylon, and can severely weaken nylon and polyester fibers. Be extremely cautious to avoid exposing your rope to battery acid or any type of acid that may be encountered in your garage or trunk of your car. Again, it is wise to keep and store your rope in a rope bag.

It is not a good idea to borrow or rent a rope, because you don't know its history. Don't lend out your rope, and keep track of its history and how long you've had it. Most manufacturers recommend keeping a rope for no longer than five to seven years even with minimal use, and no longer than ten years even if the rope has been stored and never used.

Inspect your rope by running your hand over the entire length of the sheath when coiling and uncoiling the rope. Visually inspect for excessively worn areas of the sheath, and feel for irregularities (voids, flat spots, etc.) in the core. Your rope should be retired (or cut to a shorter length) if you see the sheath is excessively worn or frayed, exposing the core, or if there are any anomalies in the core.

Marking the Middle of Your Rope

M any climbers use a black felt-tip marking pen to mark the midpoint of their rope. In 2002 the UIAA Safety Commission issued a warning based on testing done by the UIAA and by some rope manufacturers that showed the ink from some marking pens decreased the strength (more specifically, the rope's ability to hold repeated falls in accordance with the EN 892 testing standard) by as much as 50 percent. While this may seem to be a shocking figure, the UIAA president pointed out that "such a marked rope can only break in practice when the two or three centimeters, which are marked, are placed over a sharp rock edge when the rope is loaded by a fall." While this is a very remote possibility, you may want to consider other alternatives to identify the midpoint on your rope, or at least use only marking pens sold or recommended by the manufacturer of your rope. Tape is not a good option, as it can slide on the rope or, more likely, become gummy and stick in rappel and belay devices. A good option is to buy a "bipattern" rope, which is a rope that changes pattern at the middle of the rope, without a change in yarns or color. Another option is a bicolor rope, which has a color change at the midpoint of the rope. The rope manufacturer changes yarns and joins the yarns together with what is known as an "air splice" (forcing the ends to entwine around each other using extremely high air pressure). The process creates a cosmetic blemish at the yarn change, which the manufacturers say is actually stronger than continuous fibers because of the extra fibers at the splice. I've never been a fan, however, as cosmetically it looks questionable, and I've found the join to be a wear point because the fibers bulge out slightly. If you don't have a middle mark on your rope, simply start with both ends and flake the rope out until you reach the middle.

Coiling and Uncoiling Your Rope

When you buy a new rope, take extra care the first time you uncoil it to prevent kinking. The Sterling Rope company recommends the following method. Start with one end and uncoil a few strands. Then go to the other end and uncoil a few strands. Go back and forth until the entire rope is uncoiled, then inspect the rope by running it through your hands (flaking it in a loose pile) from one end to the other. Another method is to simply unroll the rope from the coil, as if pulling it off a spool, holding the rope and rotating the coil until the entire rope is stacked on the ground, keeping the rope free from any twists, then coil it with the butterfly coil method after inspection.

THE BUTTERFLY COIL

For toproping the best way to coil your rope is to use the butterfly, or backpacker, coil. This coiling method puts fewer kinks in your rope. It is also the fastest way to coil a rope, since you start with both ends and coil a doubled rope. When you're ready to set up your toprope climb, start by flaking out the rope from the ends—you'll come to the middle of the rope when you're done flaking it out. Now you can clip the middle of the rope into your anchor, toss the ends down, and your toprope climb is set up.

THE MOUNTAINEER'S COIL

Another standard coiling method is called the mountaineer's coil. This is a traditional method that makes for a classic, round coil that can be easily carried over the shoulder or strapped onto the top of a pack.

Mountaineer's Coil

Slings

In the 1960s and '70s, 1-inch-wide tubular nylon webbing was the standard sling material, tied into a loop with a water knot or double fisherman's knot. Eventually, sewn slings with bartacked stitching came onto the market, and were actually stronger than the same material tied with a knot. Sewn slings are not only stronger but also safer in that you don't have to worry about the knot loosening and coming untied. Today nylon slings are typically sold in

$^{11}/_{16}$-inch width, bartacked into 24-inch or 48-inch loops with a rating of 22 kN (4946 lb.). Climbing shops still sell 1-inch tubular nylon webbing from spools, cut to any length you wish. Nylon webbing is a slick material and should be tied with either a water knot or a double fisherman's knot. One advantage of webbing is that it can be untied and re-tied around a tree, through a tunnel, or threaded through bolt hangers for a rappel anchor. I generally only carry 1-inch webbing when I know I'll be rigging rappel anchors and leaving it behind. For

Nylon Sling Comparison. Top to bottom: 1-inch tubular nylon webbing tied with water knot (Sterling tech webbing, rated at 4,496 lb. tensile strength); 18 mm Metolius Nylon Sling, rated at 22 kN loop strength (4946 lb.); 18 mm Black Diamond Nylon Runner, rated at 22 kN loop strength (4946 lb.); $^{11}/_{16}$-inch Sterling tubular webbing, tied with water knot rated at 13 kN (3,000 lb.) tensile strength (straight pull on a single strand).

rigging and extending toprope anchors, a length of static or low-stretch rope (I prefer 10.5 mm diameter) is far more versatile than webbing, and easier to tie knots with.

Spectra slings, introduced in the late 1980s, were lighter, less bulky, and stronger than nylon. Dyneema is a more recent innovation, typically sold in various-length loops sewn with bartacked stitching in 10 mm width. Dyneema and Spectra both have almost the exact identical chemical makeup of high-molecular-weight polyethelene, which, pound for pound, is stronger than wire cable. Most experts say that the manufacturer of Dyneema consistently produces more high-quality fibers than the manufacturer of Spectra material, and most of the climbing slings on the market today are made from Dyneema.

Both Spectra and Dyneema slings are constructed from parallel fibers—very strong but with high lubricity, which means the material itself is inherently slick. That is the reason you can only buy it in sewn loops—it does not hold knots well. Do not cut a Spectra or Dyneema sling and re-tie it with a water knot!

Both Spectra and Dyneema have a lower melting point than nylon (around 300 degrees Fahrenheit for Dyneema/Spectra compared to nylon's melting point of around 480 degrees). The lower melting point, along with the inherent slipperiness, make Spectra and Dyneema slings a poor choice for tying friction hitches like the prusik, klemheist, or autoblock, compared to 5 mm or 6 mm diameter nylon cord.

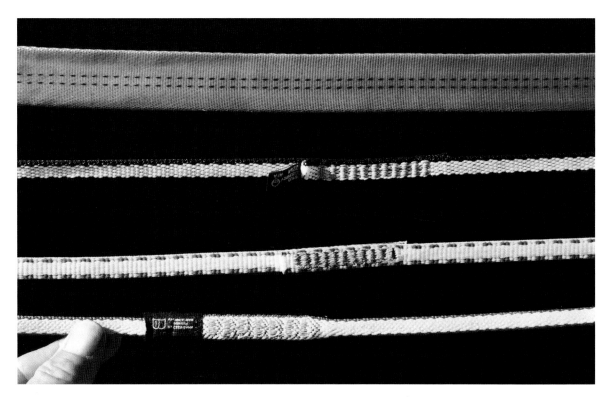

Dyneema Sling Comparison. Top to bottom: 1-inch tubular nylon webbing (for comparison); Wild Country 10 mm Dyneema sling (22 kN or 4946 lb. loop strength); Black Diamond 10 mm Dynex Runner (22 kN loop strength); Mammut 8 mm Dyneema Contact Sling (22 kN loop strength).

In a pinch, if you need to use a sling to tie a friction hitch, use a nylon one over a Dyneema or Spectra sling, because heating up a Spectra or Dyneema sling can weaken it. The newer, thinner (10 mm) Dyneema slings will work for friction hitches, and they do possess some nylon in their construction, but if they start to slide on a rope when under load, the friction will generate heat, which could potentially weaken the sling.

Both Spectra and Dyneema fibers do not retain dye and cannot be colored, so the fiber is distinctive in that it is always white. Manufacturers add a blend of nylon to Spectra and Dyneema, usually in a distinctive border pattern.

When using Spectra or Dyneema slings, think of them like a wire cable—they have almost no stretch. Avoid tying knots with them—it can be almost impossible to untie a simple overhand knot in the newer, thinner Dyneema after it has been seriously weighted. Wild Country warns that the material loses a hefty percentage of its strength (around 50 percent) when tied in a simple overhand knot or girth-hitch—a property that nylon does not possess. The best way to use a Spectra/Dyneema sling is clipped to carabiners. If using them in a sling-to-sling configuration, either basket one sling over another, or use a properly tied girth-hitch.

When buying slings for toproping, about a half-dozen single-length (24-inch) and two double-length (48-inch) slings will suffice for most situations. Any sling you purchase for toprope anchor rigging should have a minimum strength rating of around 14 kN (3,147 lb.).

Recent studies show that dirty slings are weaker than clean ones. The Mammut company suggests that "to maintain the quality and safety of your slings, you need to clean them regularly." Mammut recommends to "clean soiled slings in hand-hot water with a small amount of mild detergent or in a delicates machine cycle up to 30 degrees centigrade (86 degrees Fahrenheit). Rinse in clear water. Leave to dry in shade."

Girth-hitching two Dyneema slings together can decrease their strength by 50 percent, but for most toproping situations this is not a concern since the loop strength is 5,000 lb. to begin with.

Cord and Cordelettes

A good all-purpose cordelette is 7 mm diameter nylon cord, about an 18- to 20-foot length tied into a giant loop with a double fisherman's knot. I prefer a length that allows me to double the cordelette within the span of my outstretched arms. My favorite brand is Sterling, whose 7 mm diameter nylon cord is rated at 12.4 kN (2,788 lb.) tensile strength and tests over 5,000 pounds when tied into a loop with a double fisherman's knot.

Cordelettes made with a Spectra or Dyneema core and nylon sheath have incredibly high strength and low stretch. Pound for pound, Spectra and Dyneema are stronger than steel (and is the material used in body armor for the military), but both Spectra and Dyneema lose an appreciable amount of strength when tied with knots. Because these cords are so light and strong, with less bulk to carry, they have become popular, especially for multi-pitch climbing. The Bluewater company markets the 5.5 mm diameter Titan Cord, with a Dyneema core and nylon sheath, rated at 13.7 kN (3080 lb.). They say its "combination of high strength, low elongation, and light weight provides superior

Cord Comparison. Top to bottom: Bluewater 5 mm Titan Cord tied with triple fisherman's knot (Dyneema core/nylon sheath, tensile strength 13.7 kN or 3080 lb.); Sterling 6 mm Powercord (Technora core/nylon sheath, tensile strength 19 kN or 4,271 lb.); Sterling 7 mm Nylon Cordelette (nylon core/nylon sheath, tensile strength 12.4 kN or 2,788 lb.).

characteristics over other combinations. Dyneema does not lose significant strength with repetitive flexing and offers a huge increase in abrasion and cut resistance over other materials. BW Titan cord can be cut and sealed with a hot knife. We recommend a triple fisherman's knot for tying 5.5 Titan into loops."

In recent years "high-tenacity" cords have come onto the market, utilizing aramid fibers (namely Technora) for the core, with a nylon sheath. Aramid fiber has an exceptionally high breaking strength (stronger than Spectra or Dyneema) with low stretch and an extremely high melting point (900 degrees Fahrenheit), making it difficult to cut and melt. The Sterling 6 mm Powercord has a Technora core and nylon sheath, with a tensile breaking strength of around 19 kN (4,271 lb.); and the 5 mm Tech Cord, sold by Maxim/New England Ropes, with a 100 percent Technora core and polyester sheath, rates at a whopping 5,000 pounds tensile strength. But studies have shown that with repeated flexing aramid fibers break down more quickly (losing strength) than good old-fashioned nylon. In fact, one particular study showed that when one section of Technora fiber cord was loaded with a 40-pound weight and flexed 180 degrees over an edge 1,000 times, the material lost 50 percent of its strength, while nylon cord, in the same test, lost virtually no strength. Further research may be warranted. The big advantage of these cords is their high strength and low bulk, which is advantageous for situations like multipitch climbing.

If you use these cords, you should tie the cordelette with a triple fisherman's knot, and consider replacing them more often with high use. Keep in mind that the price tag on the high-tech cords is roughly twice as much as nylon. The bottom line is this: For an all-purpose cordelette for toproping, you can't go wrong with old-school nylon. A good choice is 7 mm diameter nylon cord.

To tie friction hitches like the prusik, klemheist, and autoblock, you'll want to use 5 mm or 6 mm diameter nylon cord (nylon core, nylon sheath). When buying this accessory cord, buy the softest, most pliable cord you can find. A stiff cord won't grip as well when used for friction hitches. Also, be aware of the difference between 5 mm nylon accessory cord (typically rated at 5.2 kN or 1,169 lb.) and 5 mm high-tenacity cord, like Bluewater Titan cord, rated at 13.7 kN (3080 lb.). You obviously would not want to use 5 mm nylon accessory cord for your cordelette!

Carabiners

Carabiners are used primarily to attach various links (like slings and rope) together in the anchor or belay chain. Locking carabiners are used in critical applications and in conjunction with belay and rappel devices. Carabiners come in a variety of shapes: oval, D-shaped, and pear-shaped.

A basic carabiner is of aluminum alloy, with a spring-loaded gate on one side. The spine of the carabiner is the solid bar stock opposite the gate. The small protrusion on one end of the gate is called the nose, and this visually tells you which way the gate opens. The basic design has a small pin on the gate that latches into a groove on the nose end. The preferable "keylock" design eliminates the pin, and the gate and bar come together in a machined notch. A wiregate carabiner simply has a wire under tension serving as the gate, which provides a wider opening because of its slim mass and eliminates "gate flutter," the vibration of a solid gate during a fall or peak loading of the carabiner.

For toproping, oval carabiners are useful for racking gear, and for use in sets of two or three for connecting the climbing rope to the toprope anchor master point. Because of their symmetry, the gates can be opposed and reversed and the carabiner configuration still retains its oval shape. Two opposed and reversed ovals can also be used in lieu of a locking carabiner at any critical junction in the anchor system, in situations where you've run out

Above, Carabiners come in a dazzling array of designs for various applications. Top row (left to right): asymmetrical D, regular D, oval, wiregate D, bentgate D. Bottom: pear-shaped locking. The most useful carabiners for toproping are ovals, Ds, and pear-shaped locking. Bentgate carabiners are used primarily for sport climbing (attached to the rope-clipping end of a quickdraw).

Left, Wiregate carabiner.

Carabiners

Two oval carabiners with the gates properly opposed and reversed.

Three oval carabiners opposed and reversed at a toprope anchor master point.

of locking carabiners and need extra security at a key point.

Locking carabiners are used for critical links and applications where it is absolutely imperative that the carabiner gate stays closed, like on a rappel or belay device, at a critical link in the anchor system, or when attaching the belayer's climbing rope to the anchor.

D-shaped carabiners have the strongest configuration, because when the carabiner is loaded on the major (long) axis, the weight naturally is loaded closest to the spine. For this reason a locking D is a good choice for a belay/rappel carabiner. A locking pear-shaped carabiner is useful for many applications because of its wide aperture on one side, and is a good carabiner to use with a Munter hitch. It is also a great carabiner to pair up for use at the toprope anchor master point. When you oppose and reverse two pear-shaped locking carabiners, the symmetry is maintained (unlike an asymmetrical D shape), and the climbing rope runs smoothly through the carabiners.

Two pear-shaped locking carabiners with the gates opposed and reversed at a toprope anchor master point.

Locking carabiners (left to right): Petzl William Triac, Petzl William Ball Lock, Black Diamond Twistlock, Black Diamond Screwgate.

The most common locking carabiner is the screwgate. The screwgate locking carabiner is just that, a mechanism with a collar that screws shut over the nose of the carabiner. I like the Petzl designs that show a red stripe (red means danger!) when the gate is unlocked. Obviously, with a screwgate locking carabiner, you have to remember to lock it, and it's an important habit to always check your locking carabiners to make sure they are locked. Check them with a close visual inspection, and also by pressing on the gate (squeeze test) for an additional safety precaution.

If you are a bit absentminded, or catch yourself occasionally not locking your screwgate carabiner, you might want to buy an autolock, or twistlock, carabiner. The twistlock design has a spring-loaded gate that locks automatically, and there are several autolocking designs on the market that have even safer mechanisms that must be manipulated (like pushing the gate upward, then twisting the gate to lock it; or pressing a button, then twisting open the gate), but some climbers find these difficult to use. Interestingly, for industrial workers in the Vertical Rope Access environment (rappelling and rope ascending on the faces of dams, buildings, and bridges), OSHA standards require autolocking carabiners, as does the tree-trimming industry.

The UIAA has determined the following

Carabiners

Every carabiner you buy should have the UIAA breaking strength ratings stamped on the spine.

Bad. Never load a carabiner in three directions as shown here.

strength ratings for a carabiner to be CE certified.
For oval carabiners:

- Closed-gate strength, major (long) axis: 18 kN (4,047 lb.)
- Minor axis strength, closed gate: 7 kN (1,574 lb.)
- Minor axis strength, gate open: 5 kN (1,124 lb.)
- For regular D-shaped carabiners:
- Closed-gate strength, major (long) axis: 20 kN (4,496 lb.)
- Cross-loading across the minor axis and loading on the major axis, gate open: 7 kN (1,574 lb.)

An important thing to remember with

carabiners is that a carabiner is only about one-third as strong if it's loaded with the gate open. It's essential, therefore, to keep a few things in mind when using a carabiner:

- Always load the carabiner in the proper direction—on the major, or long, axis.
- Do not cross-load a carabiner (on the minor axis) or load it in three directions (called tri-axial loading).
- Do not load a carabiner over an edge of rock— this can open the gate when the carabiner is loaded, and two-thirds of the carabiner's strength will be lost.

Never load a carabiner over an edge—its strength is compromised, and if the gate is forced open, the carabiner loses two-thirds of its strength.

By extending with a sling, the carabiner is now properly loaded in the strongest configuration, with the load on the spine of the carabiner.

Retire a carabiner if it shows a groove from excessive rope wear, or if it has been dropped a lengthy distance down a rock face. If the gate is sticky, washing it with soap and water and using some graphite lubricant will usually take care of the problem.

In the professional realm, the industry standard for attaching the climbing rope to the toprope anchor master point is either two locking or three oval carabiners with the gates opposed and reversed. I've always preferred three ovals because of the symmetry and wide base they present for the climbing rope. If using two locking carabiners, pick a pair of pear-shaped (not D-shaped) lockers so the pairing is symmetrical when one is opposed and reversed. I've used three ovals for thousands of client days without incident. Simply oppose and reverse the outside carabiners to the middle one. The wide

radius created by the three carabiners provides a stable platform for the rope and tends not to flip sideways as often as two locking, a situation that can pin the rope against the rock while lowering if the climber's (weighted) strand is on the outside, away from the rock.

If you do a lot of toproping, you'll see that aluminum carabiners actually wear rather quickly, developing noticeable grooves. When this happens, you should retire them. The worn-off aluminum particles also get on the rope and the belayer's hands. Using steel ovals solves both wear issues, as steel is far more durable and wears much more slowly than aluminum. One caution when using steel: If you drop them from any distance (say 20 feet or more), you should consider retiring them, as steel is more prone to micro fractures due to its metallurgical structure.

Three steel ovals with the gates opposed and reversed at a toprope anchor master point.

CHAPTER THREE

Anchoring

Rock Assessment

The first thing to think about when building anchor systems is the integrity and structure of the rock itself. Catastrophic anchor failures have occurred not because the gear placements were bad, or the rigging was flawed, but because the rock itself was unsound. Determining good rock structure and knowing what to watch out for are fundamental requirements to build safe anchors.

When placing gear, the ideal crack is what guides call "a crack in the planet," a deep fissure that runs perpendicular (i.e., at a right angle) to the plane of the rock face, cleaving a massive, solid face of granite.

In general you'll want to avoid two things: detached blocks and flakes. A detached block is just that—a chunk of rock that is not attached to the main rock structure, but is either sitting on top of the cliff like a boulder, or is part of the main rock face but completely fractured with cracks on all sides.

To assess a block, start by looking at its size. How big is it? Is it the size of your refrigerator, your car, or your house? Putting a piece of gear in the crack beneath a smaller block is a very bad idea. When the piece is weighted, it has a prying effect

outward on the block. Even large blocks can shift easily, as I've encountered when boulder-hopping around car-size blocks, only to have one shift under my body weight. Look at how the block is situated. Is it perched down low, where it cannot slide out? Does it rest on a flat surface, or is it resting on an inclined slab? Generally, be very skeptical of using detached blocks as part of your anchor system, especially smaller blocks.

Flakes should also be avoided. A flake is formed by a crack in the rock that runs parallel to the main rock face. It can be wafer thin, or several feet thick. A flake is inherently weak, since any gear placement, when loaded, will exert a prying effect outward on the structure of the flake, which can fracture if not strong enough to bear the force. In a naturally weak rock, like sandstone, a thin flake of rock can be extremely weak.

At Joshua Tree there is a climb named *Exfoliation Confrontation* that has a memorable crux where you reach underneath and undercling a flake of rock. Exfoliation is a natural process of granite formations and is the key in the formation of domes. Flakes of granite are layered, like layers of an onion, and the outer layer peels off from time to time due to the effects of weathering and gravity, exposing a new layer beneath.

Adam Radford prepares a rappel site,
Joshua Tree National Park, California.

Above, Use good judgment if anchoring to detached blocks. Avoid small ones and those situated on an inclined slab.

Left, This camming device has been placed behind a flake of rock (left). If the cam is loaded it will pry outward, potentially breaking the flake. This can cause the anchor to fail and also send the chunk of rock tumbling down onto people below.

One of the largest examples of exfoliation I've ever seen occurred in Yosemite Valley on a hot July day in 1996 at the Glacier Point Apron. An enormous flake, roughly the size of a football field and about 4 feet thick, detached from a point high on the cliff, shearing off in one gigantic piece. After a 2,000-foot free fall, the impact resulted in a massive explosion, creating a 300 mile per hour shock wave of wind that felled a thousand pine trees in a wide swath. A tourist, in line at the Happy Isles snack bar over a quarter mile away, was killed when hit by a piece of the shrapnel from the blast.

When building anchors, look with skepticism at any flake. How thick is it, and how well attached to the main rock structure or cliff face? Test its soundness by thumping on it with the palm of your hand. Does it vibrate? Is there a hollow sound? When analyzing rock structure, act like a geologist and scrutinize the rock and its various formations very carefully.

This fabricated anchor is set up only to illustrate a point. Leaning back on this rappel anchor would most likely pull this detached flake right off the cliff.

Another dangerous anchor rig using a very questionable block. The block sits on a severely inclined slab, and a pull on this toprope anchor setup may be just enough to send it sliding down the slab and over the brink.

Macro to Micro Rock Assessment

When assessing rock structure, evaluate from macro to micro. Macro is the big picture. Look at the main rock face. Is there a massive, solid rock structure? Is there a crack in the planet? Or are the cracks an intricate matrix where no real massive piece of completely solid rock exists. Are you dealing with blocks or flakes? Can you avoid using them? These are questions you need to ask. Never blindly place gear in cracks without first scrutinizing the big picture: the overall structure and integrity of the rock itself.

Microstructure is what's inside the crack you'll be using. Is the surface of the rock rotten, grainy, dirty, or flaky? Are there hollow spots or hollow flakes inside the crack itself? Microstructure can affect the integrity of your placements as much as the overall macrostructure.

This detached flake is a great example of bad rock structure.

Bad microstructure: The right side of this nut rests on a fragile flake.

Natural Anchors

Natural anchors utilize the natural features you'll find at the crag environment, such as trees, and the configuration of the rock itself. Trees are plentiful in some areas, rare in others, like in a desert environment. When assessing the reliability of a tree, there are several considerations. Is the tree alive or dead? What is the environment (dry or wet)? What is the diameter of the tree's trunk? How deeply rooted is the tree? When using a tree as part of your anchor system, a good rule of thumb is to choose a live, healthy tree with a minimum trunk diameter of 12 inches. Trees at climbing sites in the southwestern United States, because of the drier climate, are generally more reliable than trees in the Pacific Northwest or East Coast, where the climate is wetter and more humid. When setting up a toprope anchor, use two separate trees in the anchor system if possible; if only one tree is available, back it up with another gear placement or two.

The rock itself can be used for anchoring. Look for large spikes or horns of rock attached to the main rock structure to tie off as part of your anchor. A tunnel in a solid rock structure is called a thread, and is utilized by threading a sling or cord, or tying a rope, through the tunnel. Limestone is a rock type with many threads, whereas threads are a rarity in granite.

Use detached blocks with caution. They should be well situated, unmovable, and not top-heavy. Avoid using blocks resting on a slanting surface or a slab. I like to tie off the block around its entire mass, rather than using the pinch where the block touches another rock surface or where two blocks touch each other. This way even if the block shifts slightly, I still am anchored to the mass of the block.

OK. A properly girth-hitched nylon sling.

Good. A double-length (48-inch) nylon sling tied with an overhand knot makes the sling itself redundant.

Good. A figure eight follow-through knot used to tie the anchor rope directly to the tree.

A solid block tied off with a doubled cordelette using a figure eight knot, making the cordelette itself redundant.

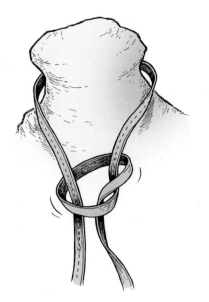

A slip hitch used to tie off a knob of rock.

A sling threaded through a tunnel with a girth hitch. This is called a "thread."

The same thread with a doubled cordelette tied with a figure eight. This adds redundancy— if one loop is cut, three loops back it up.

How to tie a slip hitch. The slip hitch can be tightened by pulling on one strand, making it more secure than a girth-hitch for tying off knobs of rock.

When tying off blocks, watch for sharp edges that may fray or cut your rigging rope, and use padding or an edge protector when needed.

A friend of mine put up a new route at Joshua Tree—a 40-foot-high sport climb with five bolts—up the face of a massive block that was a facet of a larger cliff. One day I got a phone call: "Tony's route fell down!" I didn't believe it until I walked out there and saw it with my own eyes. The gigantic block was top heavy, and had simply toppled over, with the side where Tony's route was now straight down in the dirt, leaving behind a void in the cliff the size of a small house. I got down on my hands and knees and peered underneath. I could see one of the bolt hangers! Bouldering legend Chris Sharma visited the site shortly thereafter, climbing what is now one of Joshua Tree's most difficult boulder problems, up the newly exposed overhanging face of one side of the block.

In some instances a single, bombproof natural anchor is safely used for a rappel or toprope anchor—like a 3-foot-diameter ponderosa pine tree, or a knob of rock the size of your refrigerator that's part of the main rock structure. Just make sure that your sling or rope around the anchor is redundant. For example, when rigging a rappel anchor around a massive tree, use two separate slings with two rappel rings to gain redundancy in your anchor system, at least in the rigging. When rigging a belay or toprope anchor, loop two strands of the cordelette around the tree, then tie a figure eight knot for a two-loop master point. Clip in with two carabiners, opposed and reversed, and you have redundancy in your anchor rigging (although technically, one single tree is nonredundant). Always use caution and sound judgment when using a nonredundant natural anchor.

A single, huge pine tree used for a belay anchor. Both the cord and the carabiners are doubled for redundancy in the rigging.

Nuts

The Evolution of Chockcraft

A chockstone is simply a rock wedged in a crack. Naturally occurring chockstones can be as small as a pebble or as big as a house. The notion of using a chockstone for an anchor dates back to the origins of the sport. In the late 1800s, in the British Isles, rock climbers began using natural chockstones for anchors by slinging a cord around them and attaching their rope to the sling with a carabiner. The use of artificial chockstones—called chocks, or more

commonly, nuts—began in the early 1960s, at a cliff in North Wales of all places, at a crag named Clogwyn du'r Arddu. The hike up to the crag followed a railroad track, and some ambling climber picked up a nut along the way and pocketed it. Up on the cliff he threaded a small cord through the nut before wedging it in a constriction in a thin crack. Thus the subtle art of chockcraft was born.

In American rock climbing, until the 1970s, pitons were used almost exclusively for protection and anchors. In Europe, pitons were made of soft iron, and once hammered into a crack were nearly

A selection of chocks from the 1970s. Nuts have evolved over the years but are still based on the same original basic designs.

impossible to remove and reuse. Legendary American climber John Salathe, a wrought-iron worker by trade, developed the first hard steel pitons, forged from an old Ford Model A axle, which he used for his famous ascents in Yosemite Valley during the 1940s. These high carbon steel pitons could be driven and then removed, over and over again.

Yvon Chouinard refined and innovated the design of chrome moly steel pitons from 1957 to 1965, improving on Salathe's designs with the introduction of knifeblade, horizontal (called the Lost Arrow), and angle pitons. These pitons revolutionized big wall climbing in Yosemite during the "Golden Age" of the 1960s, where hundreds of placements were required for the ultimate big wall climbs in Yosemite, like El Capitan. Once placed, they could be removed by the second, leaving the climbing route in the same condition for the next climbing team. Climbing standards in Yosemite led the world at the time.

But it came with a price. On popular climbs in Yosemite, the repeated pounding and removal of hard steel pitons began to permanently damage the cracks, leaving ugly "pin scars" every few feet

A selection of modern-day nuts.

up crack systems. Cracks were getting "beat out," and something had to be done. In Yosemite, the National Park Service actually closed down a few climbs because of piton damage.

When the great American climber Royal Robbins made a trip to England in the 1960s, he saw how effective nuts could be, and he imported the idea back to Yosemite. His 1967 ascent of *The Nutcracker*, one of Yosemite's most popular climbs, was done entirely with nuts, Royal's way of showing that nuts were a viable alternative to the destructive pitons. Climbing the route today, you'll notice there still are piton scars on the route, a testament to how slow American climbers were to embrace the new and more gentle technology of chockcraft—a big change from bashing hard steel pitons into cracks with heavy blows from a hammer.

The change was finally precipitated by the fact that many cracks were simply being destroyed. Even granite is relatively soft when compared to cold hard steel. But it wasn't until Yvon Chouinard introduced chocks to American rock climbers in his 1972 equipment catalog, and Doug Robinson espoused the virtues of nuts in his seminal treatise, *The Whole Natural Art of Protection,* that the American climbing community firmly embraced the idea of "clean climbing," a new ethic where climbing anchors were placed and removed without scarring or damaging the rock.

Today there are thin crack climbs in Yosemite where for hundreds of feet every finger jam is in an ancient piton scar, although now instead of using pitons, nuts can be slotted into the V-shaped bottom of the old pin scars.

Artificial chocks now come in a dazzling array of shapes and sizes, the largest ones capable of holding over 3,000 pounds, and the tiniest micro-nuts designed to hold body weight only. The hexentric, commonly called a hex, is a unique, six-sided nut with four distinct attitudes of placement, first introduced by Chouinard Equipment in 1971. It was followed by the Stopper in 1972, with its simple, but effective, tapered trapezoidal shape. Although there have been many new designs introduced since then, they are basically variations on a theme to these classic and timeless designs, which are still as viable today as they were more than forty years ago.

Another ingenious design, called the Tricam, invented by Jeff Lowe in 1980, is essentially a single cam that can be used either passively or actively. Since it has a tapered design, with a point on one end, it can be wedged like a nut (called a passive placement) or used like a cam (called an active placement), where a mechanical action (i.e., camming) takes place. The camming action occurs when the sling is loaded on the back, or spine, of the cam, between two rails that contact the rock on one side of the crack, creating a force that pivots like a fulcrum onto the pointed end on the other side of the crack. The design is useful for many horizontal crack situations, but can be somewhat difficult to remove with one hand or once it is weighted.

When placing a nut, or any other piece of gear for that matter, again the first thing to consider is the overall integrity of the rock itself. I can't overemphasize the importance of rock assessment. Nuts have very low holding power in soft sandstone, rotten, or flaky rock. Avoid placing nuts in cracks under or around detached blocks, or in cracks behind loose flakes. Look for "straight-in" cracks in

Piton scars on a Yosemite crack.

The classic designs of the hex (left) and the Stopper (right) have changed little since their inception in the early 1970s.

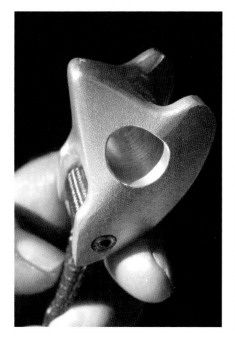

The Lowe Tricam.

Tricam in camming mode.

Tricam in passive mode.

massive rock structure, where the crack runs perpendicular to the plane of the rock face.

Once a good crack system is found, look for obvious constrictions in the crack itself. A "bottleneck" placement is found where the crack tapers drastically, and the proper size nut is fitted in the narrowing constriction.

With a basic tapered nut, like the Stopper, the preferred placement is in the narrow configuration, since this setting has the most surface contact and stability. The wider endwise configuration is an option for narrow slots and shallow cracks, but ultimately has less surface contact and generally less stability.

The typical nut placement is in a vertical crack, but horizontal cracks will work if there is a narrowing at the lip of the crack and you can slide a nut in from the side, then pull it into the constriction.

Stopper in a bottleneck placement. There is simply no way that in a downward pull the nut could be pulled through the bottleneck—something would have to give, either the rock itself or the nut or wire cable breaking.

Excellent. This Stopper placement is in good, solid rock and has flush surface contact on both sides of the nut.

Good. This endwise Stopper placement has good surface contact on both sides.

Bad. The left side of this nut lacks surface contact with the rock.

Marginal. This Stopper is in a good bottleneck, but since it lacks flush contact on the left side, a slightly outward pull will pluck it from its placement.

Good. The left side of this nut is nearly 100 percent flush, and the curve of the nut on its right side fits the curve of the crack.

Excellent. This nut has good surface contact on both sides, plus the lip on the right side of the crack protects against any outward force.

The real art of chockcraft comes into play with the more subtle placements. Look for any slight variations in the walls of the crack. When placing a nut, aim for maximum surface contact between the metal faces of the chock with the walls of the crack.

When the walls of the crack are virtually parallel sided, using the camming action of a Tricam or hex is the best option for a nut placement, although this is territory that spring loaded camming devices were designed for. When you're starting out and new to placing nuts, unless you can see an obvious, V-shaped taper in the crack, chances are you won't be able to get a reliable nut placement.

Of paramount concern when placing a nut is the direction of pull. In what direction will the chock be loaded? Most placements can withstand

a pull in only *one* direction. While the nut may be able to withstand a load of 2,000 pounds in that one direction, the slightest tug in the opposite direction might jerk the nut right out of its placement. When incorporating a nut placement into an overall anchor system, look at the ultimate direction your anchor system will be loaded, and equalize your placement in a line toward this focal point (called the master point).

Setting a nut properly is also important. Many novice climbers make a great nut placement but fail to set it properly, which makes the nut susceptible to levering out of its placement if pulled from a different angle than intended. Setting the piece is accomplished by simply applying several stout tugs in the direction the piece will be loaded, most easily

Excellent. This hex placement has near perfect flushness on both faces of the nut in a solid, straight-in crack. Loading the nut's cable will kick in the camming action of the hex.

Good. This hex is in a narrowing pocket, and both sides of the nut have good surface contact.

Bad. No surface contact on the left side makes this hex placement likely to fail with the slightest outward force.

Good. This endwise placement has great surface contact on both sides.

A nut tool is indispensable for removing chocks. Here are two models: Black Diamond (top) and Metolius (bottom).

To remove a nut with a nut tool, inspect the placement and determine its intended direction of pull, then tap in the opposite direction.

accomplished by attaching a sling to the nut with a carabiner and yanking on the sling, firmly wedging the nut in its intended placement. While this definitely makes the nut more difficult to remove, it is an important concept that many novices miss.

Carrying a nut tool, which is a metal pick designed for nut removal, facilitates "cleaning" nuts. To clean a nut can be as easy as yanking it in the opposite direction from the intended direction of pull, but be careful with recalcitrant nuts that can suddenly pop out and hit you in the face or teeth. Yanking a piece out can also send your hand bashing into the rock, scraping your knuckles. A better approach to removing a nut is to use the nut tool, giving the nut a tap opposite from the direction of loading. For larger nuts, an easy way to loosen them is to tap the nut with a carabiner, metal to metal.

To become skilled at chockcraft takes practice. Buy a selection of nuts and find a crag with plentiful crack systems at the base of the cliff. Practice rock assessment. Look for good rock structure, preferably a straight-in crack. Then look for any obvious V-shaped constrictions in the crack. If there is nothing obvious, look for any subtle narrowing of the width of the crack. Practice nut placements, aiming for maximum surface contact between metal and rock, keeping in mind the paramount importance of direction of pull. Set the nut with a sharp tug. Once set, it should not move, pivot, or wiggle in its placement when you test it with a slight tug in the opposite direction of the intended direction of loading. Practice will help you develop the knack for seeing what size nut you need for a particular placement, then selecting the proper nut and fitting it into the crack on the first try. To gain confidence quickly, take an anchoring class from a rock climbing school or hire a guide for a day of anchoring practice so you can be critiqued on your placements by a professional.

Every nut placement is different, some less than perfect, some bomber, some worthless. You should have enough knowledge to know what's good and what's not, and what constitutes a placement you can trust.

Cams

In the mid 1970s a stout, muscular fellow by the name of Ray Jardine could often be seen peering through binoculars, gazing upward at the various nooks and crannies on the walls of Yosemite Valley. With his thick beard and glasses he looked like a bird watcher, but Ray wasn't looking for birds. The bulging forearms gave it away—Ray was a climber, and he was looking for the ultimate crack: one of those perfectly straight cracks that split Yosemite's steep walls like a surgeon's incision, shooting upward for a hundred feet, uninterrupted.

Ray had invented a new technology—the spring-loaded camming device, or SLCD—that allowed him to place reliable protection in even perfectly parallel-sided cracks. When he found

The original Wild Country Friend was one of the greatest innovations in rock climbing.

his ultimate crack climb, he swore his partners to secrecy and set out on a mission: to climb the most difficult crack ever climbed in Yosemite. He named it the *Phoenix*—a fingertip- to hand-size crack on a gently overhanging wall high above Cascade Falls in the lower valley. After dozens of attempts using

Spring-loaded camming devices have become an integral part of every climber's rack.

The Metolius Power Cam has color-coded dots that help you assess your placement.

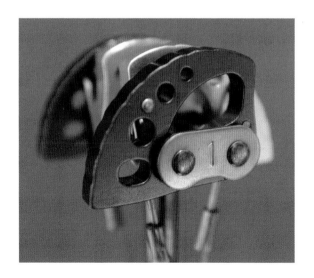

The Black Diamond Camalot was the first double-axle design.

The Metolius offset TCU (three-cam unit) works well in slightly flaring cracks.

his newfangled technology, he finally succeeded in climbing Yosemite's first 5.13. Ray called his miracle invention the "Friend," and soon the word was out. Some climbers called it "cheating," while others claimed it was "the greatest invention since the nylon rope."

Marketed by Wild Country, the Friend soon became an integral part of every rock climber's rack. Ray soon retired from climbing and, financed by his proceeds from the licensing of the Friend, went on to sail around the world, hike the Pacific Crest Trail, row across the Atlantic, and ski to the South Pole.

The idea of the SLCD, or "camming device" for short, is simple in concept yet complex in design. Jardine's original design consisted of a unit with a rigid aluminum shaft connected by an axle to four independent aluminum spring-loaded cams (called "lobes"). The cams retracted via a trigger bar that slid up and down a slot in the shaft. The unit was fitted into a parallel-sided crack with the cams retracted; when weight was applied to a sling tied into a hole in the bottom of the shaft, the cams were activated in response to the load. To keep the unit from being pulled out of the crack, a corresponding force held it in place. The downward force in the direction of the shaft was transferred outward at the cams, which generated an outward force against the walls of the crack.

The disadvantage of Ray's design was that a rigid shaft could not flex or bend in the direction of pull, an especially troubling problem for placements in horizontal cracks.

Today there is a huge array of SLCDs on the market, and the majority of these designs have flexible wire cable shafts instead of rigid ones. One of the biggest improvements since the invention of the Friend was the first double-axle design, called the Camalot, introduced by Black Diamond Equipment, which allows for a much greater range of placement of the cams. Now, in addition to units with four cam "lobes," there are TCUs (three-cam units) and offset cams (for flared cracks).

Placing an SLCD

When placing an SLCD, the first thing to consider is rock quality. SLCDs can fail if the rock is soft, brittle, or loose. They can easily pull out if placed behind a small, loose block or thin flake of rock. In solid granite, in an ideal placement, a Black Diamond Camalot can hold as much as 14 kN (3,147 lb.) Never rely on a camming device to hold in very soft sandstone, or in rotten or flaky rock. Cam manufacturer Metolius advises: "Rock fails in two basic ways: either a relatively large piece breaks off or the surface layer is crushed under the pressure of the cam lobe, allowing the cam to 'track out.' You must assess the integrity of the rock and choose the soundest possible location for your placements. Look for fractures in and around the walls of a potential placement that could denote weakness, as well as pebbles, crystals, or micro-flakes that could snap off. Be extremely suspicious of placements behind flakes or blocks."

Since they rely on friction to a certain extent, camming devices are not as strong in exceptionally slick or polished rock, or rock that is wet or icy. Again—avoid placements behind detached blocks and loose flakes—the outward expansion of the cams can generate a tremendous force that can pry the rock loose. Look for straight-in cracks in solid rock. A straight-in crack is one that runs perpendicular to the face of the rock, bisecting the rock at a right angle.

When placing a camming device, look for a section of the crack where the walls are uniformly parallel, or where they form a subtle pocket. Avoid widening cracks, where the crack is wider above the cams, as the camming device, due to its spring-loaded design, will naturally have a tendency to wiggle upward as the cam is activated. This phenomenon is known as "walking." This walking movement is most exaggerated when the piece is repeatedly weighted and unweighted, as in toproping. In a crack where the walls are uniformly parallel, or where the crack narrows slightly above the

Above, Bad. Any force applied to this Black Diamond Camalot will be converted to an outward force that can pry out and potentially break the flake of rock it's placed under.

Left, Bad. Even though the cams on this Black Diamond Camalot are within the acceptable range (right around 50 percent retracted), the widening crack above the cams will allow the cams to easily "walk" into the wider section, even with minimal loading and unloading of the device. Avoid this situation, since the cams can potentially walk to an open and unstable position.

Very good placement. All the cams have good surface contact in a solid, straight-in crack, and the cams are in the recommended range for a Camalot (50 to 90 percent retraction).

Bad. The two outside cams are not in the acceptable range for a Camalot (too wide), and they don't have flush contact with the walls of the crack.

Good. This Metolius Power Cam displays optimal green "range finder" dots in a solid, parallel-sided crack.

Poor. Although the range of retraction is acceptable, this Metolius Power Cam could easily walk up into the wider pod in the crack above the cams, rendering the placement unstable. Also, the outside right cam has poor surface contact and is too close to the edge of the crack.

Metolius recommends that in a horizontal crack, the outside cams should be placed on the bottom of the crack for maximum stability like in this Camaolt placement.

Good. This Camalot, placed in a solid horizontal slot, has all four cams tighter than 50 percent retraction with flush surface contact.

Borderline too tight. This Camalot is around 90 percent retracted. Any tighter and it may be very difficult to remove. There is also some loss of holding power in the last 10 percent (90 to 100 percent retracted) on a Camalot.

Very poor. The cams are barely retracted and nowhere near the recommended range. The piece can easily walk and might fail completely.

OK. A larger size cam would be better, but this Metolius Power Cam is in a pocket in the crack that lends some stability to the placement, even though it is borderline on the red "range finder" dots, signifying a marginal placement.

OK. This Camalot is in a slightly flaring crack, with the inside cams retracted tighter than the outside ones, although each set of cams (inside and outside) is within a suitable range and all the cams have flush contact with the rock.

Bad. The crack is way too flared for this Metolius Power Cam, and the cam on the right side has very poor surface contact with the rock.

cams, if there is any walking, the cams will not open any wider, and will stay within acceptable retraction range. As a test, grab the sling and yank and pull on it to see what walking, if any, occurs. This is an exaggerated test; when you actually use the piece the force will be more constant. Any piece will "walk" if you yank back and forth on it with enough vigor. The key point is that this is something to be aware of and watch for.

Another key to a good placement is the range of retraction on the cams. Black Diamond recommends that the Camalot be placed in the lower- to mid-expansion range (50 to 90 percent retraction), while Wild Country advises the following for its single-axle designs: "It is vitally important that all the cams make contact with the sides of the rock, preferably in the middle half of their expansion range (i.e., the cams should be one-quarter to three-quarters open)." Metolius recommends to "select the largest size cam that will fit without getting stuck. Cams should not be placed near the wide end of their expansion range. When a unit is loaded, it expands as the slack is removed from the system and the cams and rock compress. A nearly tipped-out cam won't have enough expansion left to accommodate this process. A loose cam is also more prone to walking and has little range left to adjust."

Good. This Metolius cam is in the tighter aspect of its range. Green means good to go.

Bad. The cams are too open, rendering the placement unstable. Shoot for at least halfway tight on the cams.

To illustrate what constitutes an acceptable range of retraction for the cams of a camming device, let's look at the Black Diamond Camalot in greater detail.

What is 50 to 90 percent retracted for a double-axle camming device like the Camalot? When you're looking at the Camalot without pulling on the trigger, it's at 0 percent retraction. Squeezing the trigger mechanism so that the cams are as tight as possible is 100 percent retracted. At 100 percent retracted, in a very tight placement, the Camalot will likely be very difficult to remove, and you

risk losing an expensive piece of gear. In the last 10 percent of the tightest aspect of the range (90 to 100 percent retracted), the Camalot also loses some of its holding power, another reason not to go too tight on a placement. The starting point for a good placement is at 50 percent retraction, which is when you pull the cams at least halfway tight. Looking at the base of the cams, 50 percent retraction is when the base of each cam is at a 45-degree angle relative to the vertical axis of the Camalot. If the cams are symmetrically retracted, they will be at a 90-degree angle relative to each other. A common

The same crack with two different placements. In the left-hand photo, the left outside cam has poor contact and is too close to the edge of the crack. By flipping the cam around (right photo), the gold cam now has flush surface contact with the rock. Since the inside and outside sets of cams are offset, flipping the cam one way or the other can often afford a better placement, particularly in shallow cracks in corners.

mistake novices make is to place a Camalot near the outer limit of its range (0 to 50 percent retraction). This can prove to be a very unstable placement if the unit moves at all in the crack, which can easily happen if the Camalot is placed in a crack that widens above the cams and the piece is repeatedly weighted and unweighted. Again, the optimal Camalot placement is when the cams are at least halfway tight (50 percent retracted). From the beginning position, pull the trigger mechanism until the range on the cams is half the starting size, then go only smaller and tighter from there. Scrutinize your placement after the camming device has been placed in a crack to make sure the cams are in the acceptable range.

Metolius cams have a unique color coding that assists you in assessment. The company gives this advice: "Verify that you have chosen the best size by making sure that the green Range Finder dots are lined up where the cam lobes touch the walls of the placement. Yellow dot alignment is okay too, but you must exercise more caution with the placement, because the cam will be less stable, hence more prone to walking, and it will have less expansion range left to accommodate walking to a wider position. If the cam you choose aligns in the yellow zone, the next larger size will align perfectly in the green zone. Use that cam instead, if it's still on your rack. Never use a placement in the red zone unless it's the only placement available."

Study the literature that comes with any camming device you purchase and learn what the manufacturer recommends for the acceptable range of retraction and the various placement criteria. Most manufacturers also have informative PDF files on camming device guidelines that you can download from the company's website.

To become proficient in the use of camming devices takes thought and practice. To develop confidence quickly, hire a professional guide to critique your placements. Metolius suggests to "practice placing cams in a safe venue, at ground level, before you trust your life to a cam placement. This process can teach you a lot, but written guidelines and practice are no substitute for qualified instruction. We strongly recommend that you learn to place cams under the supervision of a certified guide."

When I teach camming device placements, I first demonstrate the fundamentals, then let the student make a variety of placements with a critique on each one. Working with a guide will allow you to learn from your mistakes before venturing out on your own. Better to learn in a "ground-school" setting than on your first toprope anchor that your "Friend" was no friend at all.

Fixed Anchors

Pitons

A piton is a metal spike that is hammered into a crack for an anchor. The blade of the piton is the part hammered into the crack, leaving the protruding eye into which you can clip a carabiner. Piton anchors are something of a rarity these days, but occasionally you'll come across fixed pitons (also called pins) at the top of a crag. Follow these steps before using any fixed pin. First, assess the rock structure and look at the crack where the piton resides. Is it behind a block or flake, or is it in a straight-in crack with good structure? A good piton should be driven in all the way to the eye, and should not wiggle when you clip into it with a sling and pull on it to test it. The piton itself should not be excessively corroded or cracked. (Look closely at the eye of the piton, as this is usually where the piton will be cracked.) To effectively test a fixed pin, you really need a hammer. Give the piton a light tap—it should have a high-pitched ring to it, and the hammer should spring off the piton. If you don't have a hammer, the best test is to clip a sling into it and give it a vigorous yank in the direction you'll be loading it. You can also tap it with a carabiner or small rock. Over time, pitons

Pitons (left to right): Angle, horizontal, Leeper Z, knifeblade.

An angle piton, driven all the way to the eye—a good placement.

suffer from the vagaries of thermal expansion and contraction, particularly in winter, as water expands when it freezes, prying and loosening the piton. Often a piton can be easily plucked out with your fingers after only a few seasons. If utilizing fixed pitons as part of your toprope anchor system, always back them up, and use them with skepticism.

Bolts

The most common fixed anchor is a two-bolt anchor. Some knowledge of the history, characteristics, and specifications of bolts used for rock climbing will improve your ability to assess the reliability of bolt anchors.

In the 1960s and '70s, bolts were placed by hand drilling—an arduous process where a drill bit was inserted into a drill holder, then a hammer was used to pound on the holder to painstakingly drill into the rock. Once the hole was deep enough, a bolt, with a hanger attached, was hammered into the hole. The most common bolt during that era was the ubiquitous ¼-inch contraction bolt, called the Rawl Drive, manufactured by the Rawl Company and designed for the construction industry for anchoring in masonry or concrete. A contraction bolt has a split shaft that is wider than the diameter of the hole. When pounded into the hole, the two bowed shaft pieces are forced to straighten slightly, contracting under tension in the hole. This works fine for hard granite, but in soft rock, like sandstone, the split shaft doesn't really contract all that much, and there is little tension to keep it in the hole, resulting in very weak pullout strength (i.e., pulling straight out on the bolt).

Another problem with ¼-inch bolts is that they came in various lengths, some as short as ¾ inch long, and once placed in the rock, there was no way for future climbers to determine the length of the bolt merely by inspection.

There are two basic styles of ¼-inch Rawl Drive bolts. The buttonhead design has a mushroom-like head and is pounded into the hole with the hanger preattached. The threaded Rawl Drive has threads with a nut on the end to hold the hanger in place, a weaker configuration since the threads can weaken the shear strength of the shaft if the hanger is at the level of the threads. But more significantly, the threaded design has a serious flaw: Pulling straight out on the bolt hanger will only be as strong as the holding power of the nut on the threads, a dangerous problem if the nut is at the very end of the threads.

The shear strength on a brand-new ¼-inch Rawl Drive bolt is roughly 2,000 pounds, but the problem with contraction bolts is not shear strength but pullout strength, which varies drastically depending on the quality and hardness of the rock. In very soft sandstone the pullout strength of a ¼-inch contraction bolt is extremely low, rendering the bolt unsafe.

The buttonhead Rawl Drive bolts were also sold in 5/16-inch diameters, these being far more reliable as long as they were placed in good, hard, fine-grained granite. The 5/16-inch buttonhead, for example, has a shear and pullout strength in excess of 4,000 pounds, and for many years was the bolt of choice for first ascensionists who were hand drilling bolts. The 5/16-inch buttonhead Rawl Drive was discontinued, but the 3/8-inch buttonhead is still on the market today, with a shear strength of 7,000 pounds and a pullout strength of over 4,000 pounds in the best granite.

Probably the most disconcerting problem associated with bolts from the ¼-inch era is not the bolts themselves but the hangers. During that time, hangers made for rock climbing were manufactured primarily by the SMC company. Thankfully, the hangers are easily identified, as the "SMC" brand is stamped on them. There were two series of hangers, one good, and one very bad. The bad hangers were nicknamed the SMC "death hanger," since some of them failed under body weight after only a few seasons of exposure to the elements. These hangers are identifiable by a distinctive corrosive

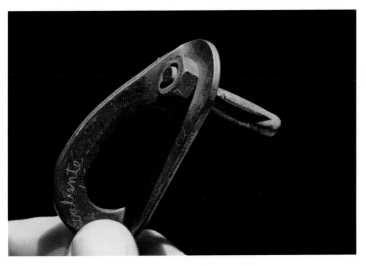

The infamous ¼-inch threaded Rawl Drive contraction bolt, complete with the SMC "death hanger." This ticking time bomb was removed and replaced from a route on Suicide Rock, California.

Buttonhead Rawl Drive contraction bolts (left to right): ⅜-, ⁵⁄₁₆-, and ¼-inch sizes.

¼-inch threaded Rawl Drive bolts with "good" (left) versus "bad" (right) SMC hangers.

⁵⁄₁₆-inch buttonhead Rawl contraction bolt with "good" SMC hanger. In a good placement in solid granite, these bolts are rated at over 4,000 pounds shear strength.

discoloration—a yellowish or bronze tint, whereas the "good" SMC hangers, made from stainless steel, show no signs of corrosion or rust and still appear silvery bright, even after twenty-five years. Another noticeable difference is in the thickness of the hangers—the "bad" hangers roughly the thickness of a dime, and the "good" ones the thickness of a quarter.

Another dangerous relic from the 1970s is the Leeper hanger. Over 9,000 of these hangers were manufactured by Ed Leeper of Colorado, and subsequently recalled because of stress corrosion problems with the metal, which rusted badly since it was not made of stainless steel. These hangers are easily identifiable due to their strange geometric shape and their rusty condition.

In the 1980s sport climbing was ushered into the United States, and climbers began to place bolts on rappel using cordless rotary hammer power drills. Since these bolts would now have to absorb numerous falls, climbers began to look for the strongest bolts available, and the standard became ⅜-inch diameter for good, solid rock (like granite) and ½-inch diameter for softer rock (like sandstone)—standards that are still prevalent today.

Although there are numerous types of bolts used in rock climbing today, the gold standard has long been the "5-piece Rawl" expansion bolt (now sold as the Powers Power Bolt). This expansion bolt has a shaft with a hex head on one end and threads on the other end (the end that goes in the hole), with a cone-shaped piece screwed onto the threads. The shaft has a two-part split sleeve, and as the hex head is tightened the cone climbs up the threads and under the sleeves, which presses the sleeves outward, "expanding" the bolt in the hole. The more you tighten it, the wider the sleeve gets. The performance and strength of the bolt relies, to a great extent, on two things: the tolerance (diameter) of the hole, and the strength of the rock itself. In good rock, the ⅜-inch Power Bolt is rated at over 7,000 pounds shear strength, with a pullout strength of roughly 5,000 pounds.

Since these bolts are really designed for the

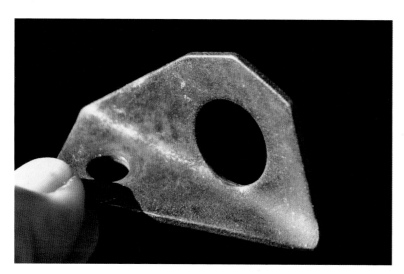

The recalled Leeper hanger can easily be identified by its unique shape and rusty condition.

Bad corrosion on a ⅜-inch-diameter threaded Rawl Drive bolt with a badly corroded Leeper hanger to match.

construction business, the Powers Fastener company lists strength ratings based on the density of the concrete they are placed in. Concrete is given a psi (pounds per square inch) rating. For example, "2,000 psi concrete" means that if you took a square inch of concrete, it would take a weight of 2,000 pounds to crush it. Hard, dense granite is analogous to 6,000 psi concrete, and soft sandstone is more like 1,000 psi concrete.

Once a bolt has been installed, it's impossible to see what's going on beneath the surface (like with the length of the bolt), and all you'll see is the head of the bolt, again making identification of the type of bolt more difficult.

If you'd like to educate yourself, peruse "mechanical anchors" on the Powers company website (www.powers.com); you'll get an excellent

tutorial on the various types of bolts and how strong they are in differing rock types.

Even if you're not an expert in mechanical engineering or in identifying bolt design and type, you should know what to watch for when inspecting a bolt anchor. An obvious red flag is rust. SMC "death hangers," Leeper hangers, homemade aluminum hangers, and any bolt or hanger with obvious signs of corrosion should never be trusted. Look closely and identify the diameter of the bolt. A ⅜-inch-diameter bolt has become the minimum standard, along with a stainless steel hanger. A bolt with threads and a nut holding the hanger in place is generally not as strong as the hex head types.

The rock should not show cracks emanating from the bolt placement—a more common problem with contraction bolts than expansion bolts.

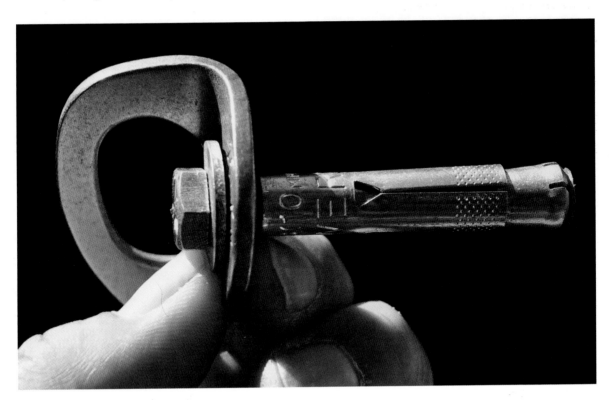

The ⅜-inch-diameter Powers "Power Bolt" expansion bolt with a stainless steel hanger has become the minimum standard for climbing anchor bolts.

³⁄₈-inch threaded expansion bolt.

³⁄₈-inch Powers expansion bolt with stainless steel Mad Rock hanger.

³⁄₈-inch stainless steel Powers bolt with stainless steel Petzl hanger, painted to match the rock color.

A well-engineered rappel anchor. Both bolts are ³⁄₈-inch stainless Powers bolts with stainless steel Petzl hangers, along with a stainless steel chain, quick link, and ring. Everything was painted before installation to match the color of the rock.

In a good placement, the hanger should be flush against the rock and should not budge or be deformed in any way. A "spinner" is a bolt that protrudes enough so that the hanger can be easily spun around 360 degrees. This generally means that when the bolt was installed, the hole was not drilled deeply enough, and the bolt contacted the bottom of the hole before the hanger could be drawn flush against the rock.

If the bolt wiggles slightly when you pull on it or the hanger is loose, and the bolt has a hex head or a nut on threads, tightening the bolt with a wrench may help, but most likely the bolt has

a problem that can't be fixed. If, while trying to tighten it you feel no increasing resistance, and it won't tighten any further, then the bolt has serious problems—usually this means the tolerance (diameter) of the hole is too big for the bolt, or the rock is too soft.

As someone who has replaced many bolts over the years, I can tell you that any ¼-inch bolt should be considered suspect, particularly in less than perfect rock. I've plucked out many ¼-inch contraction bolts that came out with about the same resistance as a nail being pulled out of plywood. To replace a ¼-inch bolt, the best method is to pry it out of its

All these old bolts at Joshua Tree were replaced with brand-new stainless steel hardware, courtesy of the ASCA.

This rack has a good assortment of both nuts and camming devices.

hole, then re-drill the same hole to a ½-inch diameter and install a ½-inch-diameter stainless steel Powers Power Bolt (10,000 lb. shear strength) with a stainless steel hanger. I like to paint the hanger (before I install it) the same color as the rock so that the bolt is visually unobtrusive. It's a good feeling to replace a ticking time bomb with a solid anchor that will last a lifetime.

The American Safe Climbing Association (ASCA) has been very active in donating the necessary (and expensive) hardware to climbers, like myself, who take on the task of upgrading unsafe bolt anchors with modern, stainless steel bolts and hangers. If you'd like to support and donate to the ASCA, you can contact them at www.asca.org.

Toproping Rack

For toproping, you don't need the tiniest nuts and camming devices designed for aid climbing or body-weight placements; you'll want gear with an individual minimum breaking strength of at least 10 kN (2,250 lb.).

Buying more large nuts (like hexes) will save you money if you're on a budget, but camming devices will prove more versatile. Many experienced climbers rarely carry a full range of hexes these days.

Here is an example of a rack that will allow you to rig a toprope anchor system in most situations:

1 set of wired nuts from 0.5 to 2 inches (e.g., Black Diamond Stoppers, sizes 4–12)

1 set of hexes or tricams from 1 to 2.5 inches (e.g., Black Diamond Hexes, sizes 5–8 , Camp (Lowe) Tricams, sizes #2–4)

1 nut tool

1 set of camming devices from 0.4 to 4 inches (e.g., Black Diamond Camalots .4, .75, 1, 2, 3), plus doubles on 1 and 2

6 single-length (24-inch) slings

2 double-length (48-inch) slings

2 cordelettes (18 to 20 feet of 7 mm nylon cord)

1 length of low-stretch rope for rigging (10.5 mm by 80 to 100 feet)

10 to 12 carabiners

4 to 6 locking carabiners

Basic Toprope Anchor Systems

The RENE Principle

The RENE principle is a simple, easy to remember acronym used for evaluating a toprope anchor system. RENE stands for Redundancy, Equalization, and No Extension.

Redundancy means there is no place in the anchor system where you are relying on any one single piece of equipment, be it a strand of cord, sling, or carabiner—in other words, there is always a backup. For bolt anchors the minimum would be two bolts, preferably ⅜-inch diameter. For toprope gear anchors utilizing nuts and camming devices, a good minimum number, and the industry standard for professional guides, is three pieces of gear. Clipping a climbing rope into the anchor system's master point with a single, locking carabiner would not be redundant. With regard to rock structure, if the integrity of the rock is at all in question, using two different rock structures (e.g., two different crack systems) would add redundancy.

Equalization means that when the load is applied to the master point on the anchor system, the weight is evenly divided onto all the various components in the anchor. An anchor can be pre-equalized, which means that the system is tied off to accept a force in one specific direction (most often the case in toproping), or self-equalizing, meaning

the anchor is rigged to adjust to loading within a range of direction changes.

No Extension means that if any one piece in the anchor fails, there will not be any significant amount of slack that develops before the load can be transferred to the remaining pieces. This is a key concept to remember when rigging toprope anchors that are extended over the edge, as oftentimes the anchors are a significant distance away from the master point. A good rule of thumb is to limit any extension in your anchor system to no more than half the length of a single-length (24-inch) sling.

Principles of Equalization

Pre-Equalized: The Cordelette System

The cordelette system is a pre-equalized system, meaning that once you tie off the cordelette in the anticipated direction of loading, if the load shifts slightly in any direction, all the load goes onto one placement (albeit with minimal extension), unlike a self-equalizing system that adjusts with changes in the direction of the loading. For toprope anchor systems, you can, in most cases, readily determine the direction your anchor system will be loaded in, so complex self-equalizing rigs are not required. The cordelette system is essentially a

Eric Hörst works up a thin, unprotectable crack on a toprope at Great Falls in Virginia.

system of backups. If one piece fails, the load transfers instantly to the remaining pieces with minimal shock loading, since the rigging limits extension.

The beauty of the pre-equalized cordelette system is that it is easy to remember and simple to rig. The cordelette is fairly versatile in that it can be used to rig two, three, or four placements. The most common fixed anchor you'll encounter is a two-bolt anchor. An easy and bomber rig is to start by doubling the cordelette, then clipping the doubled strand into both bolts with locking carabiners. Pull down between the bolts, gather all the strands together, and tie a figure eight loop. This gives you four strands of cord at the master point.

To rig three or four placements, clip the cordelette into all the placements, then pull down between the pieces and gather all the loops together. I like to clip a carabiner into all the

Simple two-bolt anchor rigged with a Tech cord (5,000 lb. tensile strength) cordelette. The cordelette is doubled to start with, producing four strands at the master point loop, and the climbing rope is clipped into three oval carabiners opposed and reversed.

Demonstration of pre-equalized cordelette with three anchor placements, tied with a 7 mm nylon cordelette. A clove hitch has been tied to the top left piece to keep the double fisherman's knot away from the end loops. This is a simple and effective rig as long as the direction of load is predetermined, which is most often the case when toproping.

Four-piece anchor pre-equalized with 6 mm Powercord cordelette. The two locking carabiners are opposed and reversed.

gathered loops and pull in the anticipated loading direction, then tie a figure eight knot with the carabiner attached to help even out all the strands. If you find yourself coming up a bit short on enough length to tie off all the loops with a figure eight, an overhand knot will take up less cord, and even though it's a slightly weaker knot, this is not a factor since you'll have at least three or four loops at your master point. Another trick is to take a regular length (24-inch) sling and clip it into the piece that's farthest away from you—this will give you more length to work with on the cordelette.

Rigging a Cordelette

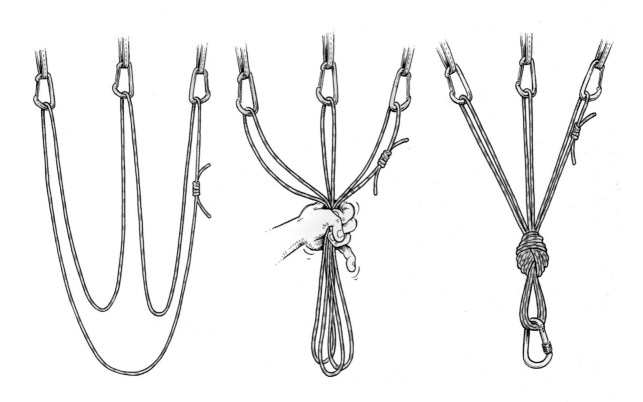

An 18- to 20-foot-long cordelette is usually long enough to equalize three or four anchor points, as long as they are not spaced too far apart. Use a sling or two if necessary to get all the carabiners you'll be clipping into within a workable range. Clip a single strand of the cordelette into each carabiner, then pull down between the pieces and gather the loops (with three pieces you'll have three loops). Clipping a carabiner into the loops before you tie the knot will make it easier to equalize all the strands. Tie a figure eight knot to create your master point, which should be roughly 3 to 4 inches in diameter. If you don't have enough cord to tie a figure eight, an overhand knot takes up less cord.

The drawback of the cordelette system (left) is that if the direction of the anticipated load changes, one piece in the anchor takes all the load (right). Think of the cordelette system as a system of back-ups: If the one piece that is loaded fails, the load goes onto the next piece with relatively minimal extension in the system. For toproping anchors, since the load on the anchor system is relatively low, the cordelette system has the advantage of being easy to use and simple to rig, negating any potential for shock loading.

Self-Equalizing Systems

THE SLIDING X

The sliding X (aka magic X) is a simple way to equalize two anchor points with a sling, creating a mini-anchor system that adjusts as the load shifts in direction. In scrutinizing the overall anchor system, if I use a sliding X between two pieces, I count this as only one placement as far as redundancy is concerned, because it is only one sling. However, by equalizing two placements that can adjust to slight shifts in direction, you create one more inherently bomber piece.

If using the sliding X with a long sling (like a sewn, 48-inch double-length sling), you can minimize extension by tying overhand knots just above the clip-in point. This allows the system to adjust, but limits any extension if one piece fails.

To set up a simple self-equalizing anchor system from two bolts, you can use two single-length slings together with a sliding X, creating a redundant rig with minimal extension.

Rigging a Sliding X

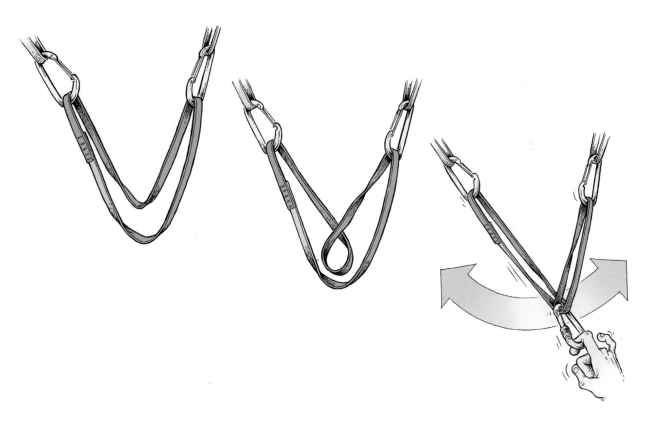

Using a single sling you can create a self-equalizing system that adjusts with changes in the direction of the loading.

When rigging a sliding X, make sure you clip into the loop you've created by twisting the sling.

When the loops are of unequal length on a sliding X rig, you can limit extension (and potential shock loading) by tying an overhand knot on the longer end, just above the carabiner. But if you're using a Dyneema sling, any knot will reduce the breaking strength almost in half.

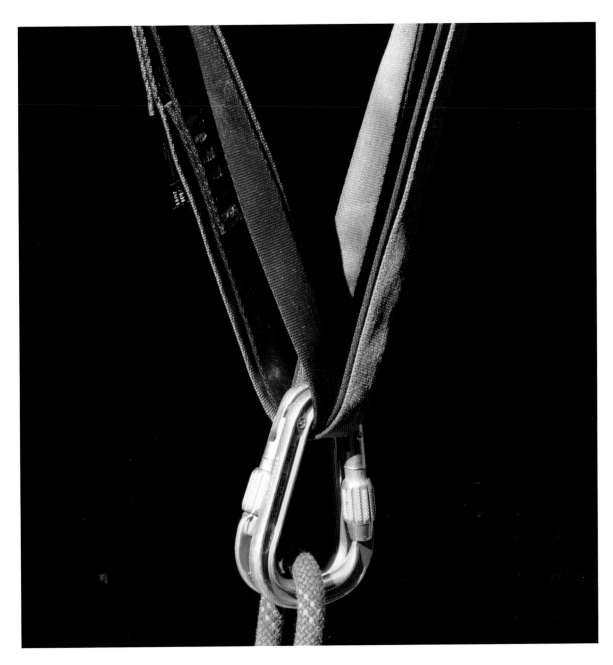

A simple two-bolt anchor can be rigged with a sliding X using two slings and two locking carabiners at the master point for a redundant, self-equalizing system. With a two-bolt anchor I always use locking carabiners on the bolt hangers too. The drawback of this rig is that if one bolt were to fail, the system would extend to the length of the slings. As a general rule of thumb, limit the maximum extension in your anchor system to half the length of a single-length (24-inch) sling.

THE QUAD

The quad is a great system to use for equalizing two-bolt toprope anchors. It gives you near perfect equalization with minimal extension and great strength. To rig the quad, start by doubling your cordelette, then grab the middle with your fist. Tie an overhand knot on each side of your fist, and you're ready to rig. Clip the double-strand

A two-bolt anchor rigged with a 7 mm cordelette and the quad system.

Detail from photo on left. The cordelette is clipped directly to the bolt hangers with locking carabiners, bypassing the cheap hardware store lap links (which only rate at around 1,000 pounds).

loops into the bolts with locking carabiners, then clip only three of the four strands at the master point, leaving one loop outside your master point carabiners. This ensures that if one bolt fails, you are clipped into a pocket on the master point.

Detail of quad rig master point with three ovals opposed and reversed.

Detail of quad rig with two locking carabiners opposed and reversed.

THE EQUALETTE

The equalette rig gives you four strands, or "arms," running from the master point to the various pieces in your anchor matrix. These four arms can be tied to the pieces with figure eights, clove hitches, or double loop knots like the double loop eight or double loop bowline.

To tie an equalette rig, form a U shape with

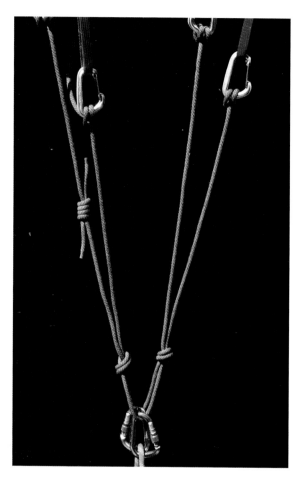

The equalette rigged with a 7 mm nylon corde-lette. This is a versatile system to use for equal-izing three or four placements, giving you re-dundancy, equalization, and no extension. The only drawback is in its complexity and the fact that it does not have one singular master point to clip into. Here the equalette is rigged to four placements, using the various "arms" of the cordelette attached with clove hitches for easy adjustment.

Detail of the equalette master point using two locking carabiners opposed and reversed.

your cordelette and grab the bottom of the U, positioning the fisherman's knot on the cordelette about 18 inches away from the bottom of the U. Tie an overhand knot on both sides of your fist, about 10 inches apart.

At the master point, you'll have two separate loops. Clip into each loop with a separate locking carabiner.

Detail of equalette master point rigged with a Dyneema sling. Tying an overhand knot in a Dyneema sling reduces its strength by 50 percent; it's better to use a 7 mm nylon cordelette when rigging the equalette, as you'll be tying lots of knots.

Detail of an equalette toproping rig tied with a doubled cordelette for a two-bolt anchor.

Vectors

A vector is a quantity that incorporates both direction and magnitude. Picture a tightrope walker balancing out on the middle of a wire. If he weighs 200 pounds, the load at each end where the wire is attached will be roughly 1,000 pounds. Why is this? When two anchor points are equalized, as the angle of the wire, sling, cord, or rope approaches 180 degrees, the forces at the anchor points increase drastically. When the angle is narrow, the load is distributed at around 50 percent to each anchor.

Keep this in mind when you build toprope anchor systems. If the angle between two anchor points reaches 120 degrees, you'll load each anchor at 100 percent. Strive to keep all the angles under 60 degrees so you'll be splitting the load roughly 50/50. A good rule of thumb is to always keep the angles under 90 degrees. Also, avoid rigging a sling between two anchors in a triangular configuration (called the American Triangle), which, even at 90 degrees, places 1.3 times the force at each anchor point. An American Triangle rigged at 120 degrees would almost double the load at each anchor point!

American Triangle

Load per anchor with 100 lb. of force

Bottom Angle	V Rigging	Triangle Rigging
30 degrees	52 lb.	82 lb.
60 degrees	58 lb.	100 lb.
90 degrees	71 lb.	131 lb.
120 degrees	100 lb.	193 lb.
150 degrees	193 lb.	380 lb.

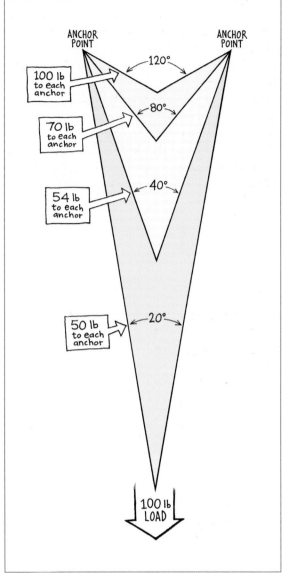

ANCHOR POINT   ANCHOR POINT

120°

100 lb
to each
anchor

80°

70 lb
to each
anchor

40°

54 lb
to each
anchor

20°

50 lb
to each
anchor

100 lb
LOAD

The American Triangle rigged at a rappel anchor. Avoid rigging with a triangle configuration—it adds unnecessary forces to your anchor points. Stick to a V configuration for lower loads.

This diagram illustrates how a 100-pound load is distributed between two anchor points at various angles. Keep the angle between two anchors as narrow as possible, striving to keep it under 60 degrees. At 120 degrees the load is 100 percent at each anchor! Think of 0 to 60 degrees as ideal, 60 to 90 degrees a caution zone, and over 90 degrees a danger zone.

Basic Knots

Loop Knots

Loop knots are tied by taking two strands of rope (called a bight) and wrapping them back over themselves so that the knot does not slide, or by taking the end of the rope and tying it back over the standing part so the knot does not slide. Loop knots are used to clip the rope into a carabiner, or to tie around an object.

Overhand Loop

This is the simplest knot you can tie to form a loop. It requires less rope to tie than the figure eight, which makes it useful on cordelettes when you don't quite have enough length to tie the master point with a figure eight loop. For most applications, however, the figure eight loop is superior because it tests about 10 percent stronger than the overhand loop and is easier to untie in small-diameter cord.

Knot Terminology

Bend: Two ropes tied together by their ends.

Bight: Two strands of rope where the rope is doubled back on itself.

Load strand: The strand of the rope that bears all the weight.

Hitch: A knot that is tied around another object (such as a carabiner or rope).

Standing end: The part of the rope that the end of the rope crosses to form a knot.

Tag end: The very end of a rope, or the tail end that protrudes from a knot.

Lisa Hörst topropes Juliet's Balcony *above the Potomac River at Great Falls, Virginia.*
STEWART M. GREEN

Overhand loop.

Figure Eight Follow-Through

This is the standard knot for tying the rope to your harness. It can also be used to tie an anchoring rope around an object like a tree or through a tunnel. Tie it with a 5-inch minimum tail, and tighten all four strands to dress the knot.

Finished overhand loop.

A properly tied figure eight follow-through knot.

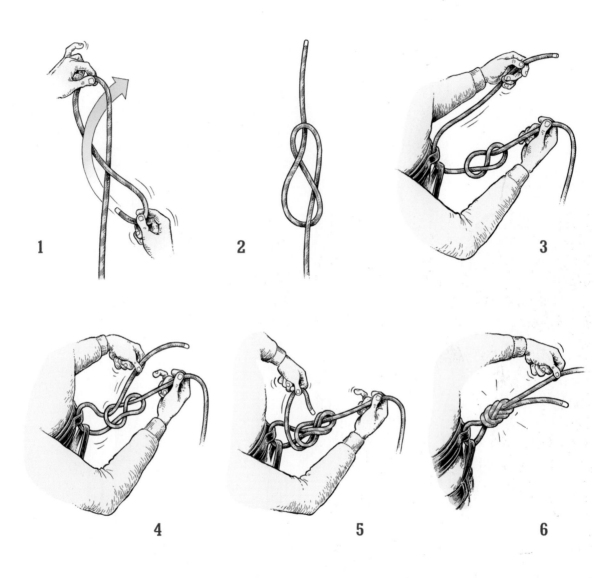

1

2

3

4

5

6

Check your harness manufacturer's guidelines for information on how to properly tie the rope to your harness. For harnesses with belay loops, you generally follow the same path as the belay loop, which goes through two tie-in points on the harness. Tie the figure eight so that its loop is about the same diameter as your belay loop. The figure eight knot does not require a backup knot.

Figure Eight Loop

Another standard climbing knot, the figure eight loop is used for tying off the end of a rope, or for tying a loop in the middle, or "bight," of a rope. It is also commonly referred to as a "figure eight on a bight."

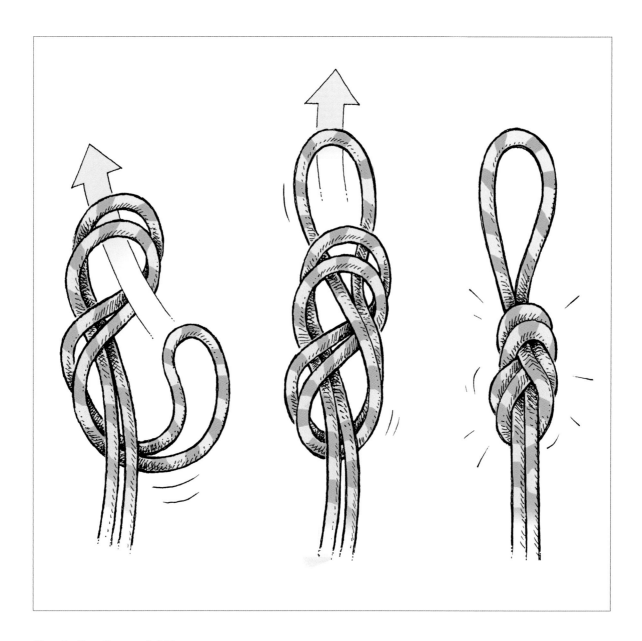

How to tie a figure eight loop.

Finished figure eight loop clipped to an anchor.

Bowline

If you were a Boy Scout, you learned this knot with the saying "the rabbit comes up through the hole, around the tree, and back down through the hole." The bowline is very useful to tie the rope around something, like a tree, block of rock, or tunnel in the rock. It is important to note that a bowline knot requires a backup, as weighting and unweighting the knot easily loosens it. Always tie half of a double fisherman's knot to back it up. One advantage of the bowline is this same feature—it is very easy to untie after it has been weighted.

The bowline knot with fisherman's backup.

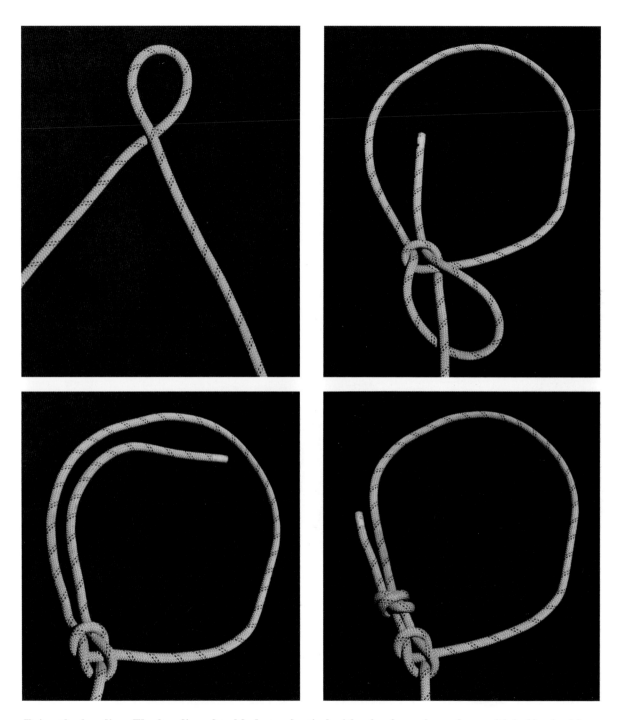

Tying the bowline. The bowline should always be tied with a backup, shown here with half a double fisherman's for the backup knot (final photo).

Re-threaded bowline. Tie a regular bowline, but leave the tail long enough to go all the way back around the object you're tying around, then retrace the start of the knot, like you would on a figure eight follow-through, finishing with a fisherman's backup. This is a great knot to use for tying a rope around a tree or through a tunnel, because you end up with two loops, adding strength and redundancy to your rigging.

Knots for Webbing

Nylon webbing is a slick material that should be tied with caution: There have been many accidents where poorly tied knots in nylon webbing have failed. The two recommended knots for tying nylon webbing into a loop are the water knot (also known as the ring bend) and the double fisherman's knot (also known as the grapevine knot). When tying the water knot, your finished tails should be a minimum of 3 inches in length. It is important you tighten the water knot properly, as it has a tendency to loosen if tied slackly in a sling that is being used over time.

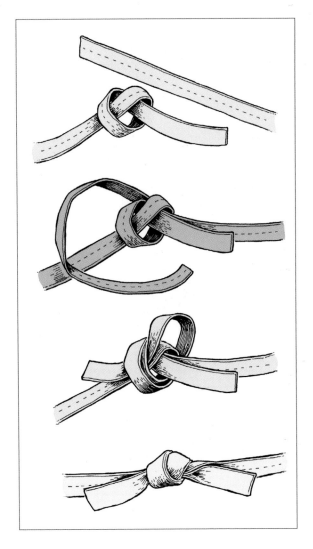

Tying the water knot (ring bend).

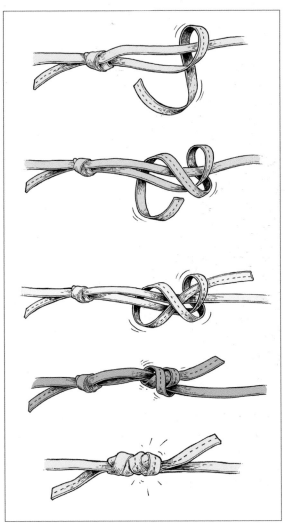

Tying nylon webbing with a double fisherman's (grapevine) knot.

Why would you even use nylon webbing tied with a knot as opposed to a sewn runner? A sewn nylon runner is stronger than the same material tied with a knot. The answer is for rappel anchors when you tie slings around a tree or through bolt hangers. It is also sometimes useful to untie the knot, thread it through something (like a tunnel), and re-tie it.

The double fisherman's knot is also a good knot to use to tie nylon webbing into a loop, although it does require more length of material to tie and is very difficult to untie after it has been seriously weighted.

The water knot.

Bends

A bend is a knot that joins two ropes or lengths of cord together. These knots are used to tie your cordelette into a loop, and also to tie two ropes together for toproping or rappelling.

Figure Eight Bend

A variation of the figure eight follow-through, this knot can be used to tie two ropes together. It has superior strength and is easy to untie after it has been weighted. It is simply a retraced figure eight. On 9-mm to 11-mm-diameter rope, tie it with the tails a minimum of 5 inches long.

The figure eight bend.

Double Fisherman's Knot

This is the preferred knot to use for joining nylon cord into a loop to make a cordelette. It is also a very secure knot to tie two ropes together for a double-rope rappel, but can be difficult to untie.

The double fisherman's knot.

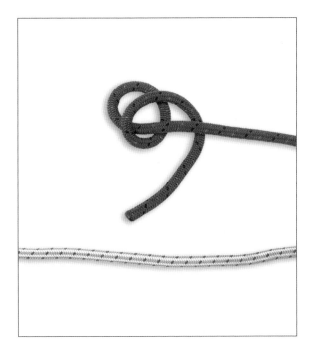 

Tying the double fisherman's knot (aka grapevine knot). When tying 7 mm nylon cord, leave the tails about 3 inches long.

Triple Fisherman's Knot

For 5 mm- and 6 mm-diameter high-tech cord (i.e., Spectra, Dyneema, Technora), a triple fisherman's knot tests slightly stronger than the double fisherman's.

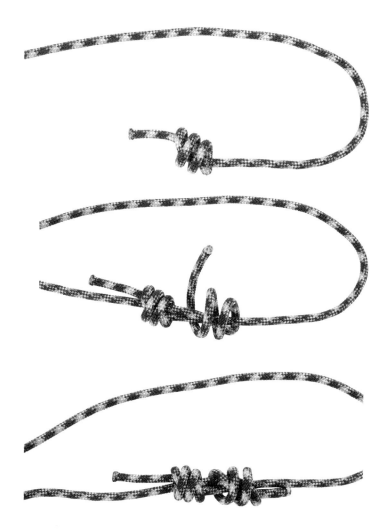

To tie a triple fisherman's, make three wraps before feeding the cord back through.

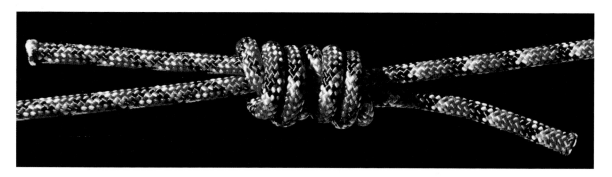

The triple fisherman's knot.

Hitches

The clove hitch is used to fasten a rope to a carabiner. A friction hitch is a knot tied with a cord or sling around another rope, utilizing friction to make the knot hold when it is weighted, but releasable and moveable without untying when it is unweighted.

Clove Hitch

The clove hitch is tied around the wide base of a carabiner. The beauty of the clove hitch is easy rope-length adjustment without unclipping from the carabiner, making it a truly versatile knot for anchoring purposes: for anchoring a belayer, tying off an anchoring extension rope, or tying off the arms of a cordelette.

Get in the habit of tying the load-bearing strand on the spine side of the carabiner, and you'll ensure that you're loading the carabiner in the strongest configuration. Make sure you tighten the clove hitch properly by cranking down on both strands, and you're good to go.

Tying the clove hitch.

Prusik Knot

A prusik knot is used for rope ascending and as a component in many rescue systems. It can be loaded in either direction. To tie a prusik, first make a "prusik cord" out of a 4.5-foot length of 5 mm–or 6 mm–diameter nylon cord tied into a loop with a double fisherman's knot. Buy the softest, most pliable nylon cord you can find, because a softer cord will grip best. To tie the prusik, simply make a girth-hitch around the rope with your cord, then pass the loop of cord back through the original girth-hitch two or three more times. Dress the knot to make sure all the strands are even and not twisted—a sloppy friction hitch will not grip as well. Test the knot before using it. A thinner cord will grip better, but below 5 mm in diameter the cord will be too weak for many rescue applications. To slide the prusik after it has been weighted,

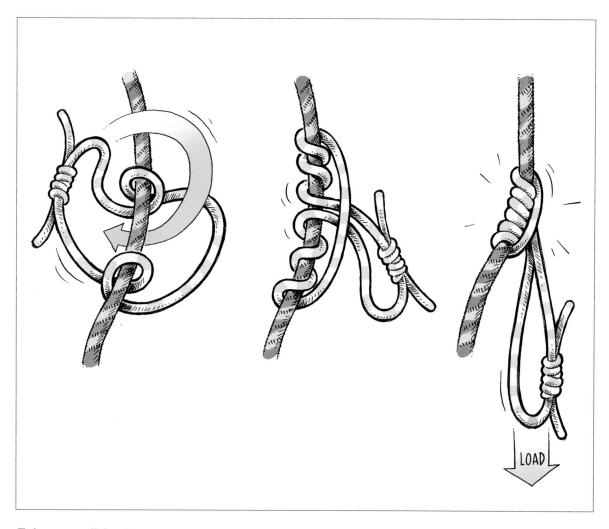

Tying a prusik knot.

loosen the "tongue," which is the one strand oppo-site all the wraps.

Tests on various friction hitches reveal that the prusik consistently has the most holding power in a wide array of cord and rope combinations, so use the prusik in scenarios (like 3:1 raising systems) where it will be loaded with more than body weight.

A four-wrap prusik.

Klemheist Knot

This is another useful friction hitch that is quick and easy to tie, and is a good choice as a rope-ascending knot, or if you're forced to use a sling rather than a piece of cord to tie a friction hitch. If using a sling, pick a nylon one over a Spectra or Dyneema sling, because it grips better and is less susceptible to weakening if it gets hot (nylon has a higher melting point). Four wraps of 6 mm cord tied on a single 10 mm-diameter rope usually work well. After the hitch has been weighted, loosen the tongue (the one strand opposite all the wraps) to slide it more easily. If tied the opposite way, with the tongue at the base of the wraps, it is commonly referred to as the hedden knot. The hedden knot (aka the kreutzklem knot) is normally tied with just two wraps. It has great holding power, but is harder to unlock than the klemheist once it has been weighted.

Tying the klemheist knot.

Autoblock

Sometimes called the "third hand," the autoblock is used to back up your brake hand when lowering someone, or to back up your brake hand when rappelling. Tie it with your loop of 5 mm- or 6 mm- diameter nylon cord wrapped three or four times around the climbing rope. When I tie it on a single strand of 10 mm-diameter climbing rope (as in a lowering situation), I usually make four wraps. For a rappel backup on a doubled 10 mm rope, I usually go with three wraps.

The autoblock.

Belaying from the Base

On a beautiful summer's day in 1865, a party of seven climbers, led by Edward Whymper, stood jubilant on the summit of Switzerland's Matterhorn, looking down on the tiny gingerbread town of Zermatt far below. Theirs was the first ascent of the icy pyramid—the greatest achievement in alpine climbing at the time, and for Whymper, perhaps the sweetest victory, after a dozen attempts. On the descent the climbers' euphoric revelry was suddenly interrupted by a slip and a fall. All the climbers were tied together into the same rope, which summarily broke, sending four climbers plunging to their death. The three survivors were saved from a tragic fate by the weak rope, since they were unanchored and had no belay.

Belaying is the act of properly using the climbing rope to safeguard a climber. In the event of a fall, the belayer locks off the rope to stop the fall. The belayer's responsibility is to manage the slack in the rope, always maintain a brake hand on the brake strand of the rope, and stop a fall by using the proper brake hand position to create maximum friction at the belay device. Belaying is a big responsibility, and if you take on the task you should be competent and alert, and you should know the proper safety checks and belay signals.

Belay Devices

I began climbing before the advent of the belay device. Back in the 1970s we used the "hip belay" technique to catch a fall, which was simply wrapping the rope around your waist to generate enough friction to stop a fall. Catching a climber on a big "whipper" was painful indeed, and I often ended a hard day of climbing with a black streak singed across the back of my waistline.

Today there is a wide variety of belay devices available. The most commonly used belay device is a tube or slot device (with two slots so it can be used for both belaying and rappelling on a doubled rope). A bight of rope is threaded through one of the slots in the belay device and clipped into a locking carabiner attached to the belay loop on the front of the belayer's harness. When the two strands of rope (one going to the climber, one to the belayer's brake hand) are held parallel, in front of the belay device, there is little friction, but when the brake strand is held at a 180-degree angle relative to the strand going to the climber, the device affords maximum friction, making it relatively easy to hold the force of a falling climber.

Learning the proper hand movements is key to becoming a safe belayer. There are many techniques

Jen Bauer belays Jess Meiris using a slingshot belay on Solar Slab at Red Rock Canyon Open Space, Colorado.

The hip belay is the most elemental form of the belay. To take in rope, start with the brake hand at your hip, and the guide, or "feel," hand extended.

To take up slack, the brake hand goes out as the guide hand comes in.

The guide hand reaches above the brake hand and pinches the rope . . .

. . . so that the brake hand can slide back.

In the event of a fall, the brake hand brings the rope in front of the waist for maximum friction.

Black Diamond ATC belay device.

acceptable for a safe belay, and they all have this in common: They effectively manage the slack, maintain a brake hand on the brake strand side of the rope, and generate enough friction to stop a fall and safely lower a climber.

Over the last decade advances in technology have allowed manufacturers to produce thinner ropes, and belay devices have evolved along with the ropes. When buying a belay device, check the manufacturer's specifications and make sure it's appropriate for the diameter of your climbing rope. The most popular tube device is the Black Diamond ATC (tongue in cheek for Air Traffic Controller), which also comes in a more versatile version with teeth on one side (the ATC XP) that gives the belayer two options: a regular friction mode when the brake strand is on the non-teeth side, or roughly twice the amount of friction when the brake strand is on the teeth side.

Black Diamond ATC XP in high-friction mode with the teeth on the braking side.

Black Diamond ATC Guide in autolocking mode.

Petzl Grigri in lowering mode.

Trango Cinch in lowering mode.

Several manufacturers make tube devices that also have an autolocking mode, namely the Black Diamond ATC Guide and the Petzl Reverso, making them versatile choices that can be used for both belaying and rappelling in the regular mode, or in the autolocking mode for belaying directly off the anchor.

Self-locking assisted braking devices (ABDs) like the Petzl Grigri and Trango Cinch work by a camming action and pinching of the rope rather than friction; but the device must be quickly loaded to lock, like a seat belt. ABDs have a handle that must be opened to release the tension, as when lowering a climber, in conjunction with the brake hand maintaining friction and controlling the speed of the lower. These devices are far from foolproof, however, and many accidents have occurred with ABDs. The cardinal rule to remember with ABDs, and any belay device is this: Never take your brake hand off the rope! The ABDs are very useful for direct belays when belaying from the top of the cliff.

With any belay device, read the manufacturer's guidelines carefully, and seek proper instruction from a certified guide or experienced climber if you have any doubts about how to use the device or the proper technique to use when belaying with the device. Someone's life is, literally, in your hands, and it's your responsibility, if you're the belayer, to know what you're doing.

Standard Climbing Signals

A methodical safety check, along with proper use of the universal climbing signals are integral parts of a safe climb. Ambiguity in the use of climbing signals has led to many tragic accidents, simply because of lack of communication between the climber and belayer. One infamous tragedy occurred at a popular ice climbing area, in a toprope setup, when the climber reached the top of the climb (at the top of the cliff) and the anchor. The climber yelled, "I'm OK!" but the belayer thought he heard, "Off belay." The belayer unclipped the rope from the belay device and took the climber off belay, thinking he was going to walk off the top. The climber leaned back to be lowered, and fell to his death.

On a yo-yo toprope climb it's important to be vigilant at the transition from the climb up to the lower down. This is where most accidents due to improper communication and climbing signals occur. There should be no ambiguity. I always hold onto the strand of rope that goes back down to my belayer until I am sure he or she has heard my command and is in the brake position and ready to hold my weight. In most cases you'll be within visual contact, so in addition to hearing the verbal commands, you'll want to look down over your shoulder and visually verify that the belayer is being attentive, with his or her hand in the proper brake position, alert and ready to lower you safely. In situations where you are climbing with other parties around you, it's best to include your partner's name in the signal (e.g., "Off belay, Bob.") to prevent confusion.

Here are the standardized climbing signals that I've used for almost thirty years in my climbing school:

On belay?: Climber to belayer, "Am I on belay?"

Belay on: Belayer to climber, "The belay is on."

Climbing: Climber to belayer, "I'm beginning the climb."

Climb on: Belayer to climber, "Go ahead and start climbing; I have you on belay."

Up rope: Climber to belayer, "There is too much slack in my rope. Take up some of the slack." (Too much slack in the belay rope will mean a longer fall. Remember that rope stretch also contributes to the total distance of a fall, especially when there is a lot of rope out in a toprope scenario.)

Slack: Climber to belayer, "Give me some slack, the rope is too tight."

Continued on next page

Tension (or Take): Climber to belayer, "Take all the slack out of the rope and pull it tight; I am going to hang all my body weight on the rope." (This could be a situation where the climber simply wants to rest by hanging in the harness while weighting the rope, or a toprope situation where the climber is getting ready to be lowered back down a climb.)

Tension on (or I've got you): Belayer to climber, "I've taken the rope tight, and my brake hand is now locked off in the brake position, ready to hold all your weight."

Lower me: Climber to belayer, "I'm in the lowering position (feet wide, good stance, sitting in the harness, weighting the rope, and leaning back), and I'm ready to be lowered."

Lowering: Belayer to climber, "I'm proceeding to lower you."

Off belay: Climber to belayer, "I'm safe. You can unclip the rope from your belay device and take me off belay." (Never take someone off belay unless you hear this signal. The universal contract between belayer and climber is that the belayer must never take the climber off belay unless the climber gives the belayer the "off belay" command.)

Belay off: Belayer to climber, "I've unclipped the rope from my belay device and have taken you off belay."

That's me!: Climber to belayer, "You've taken up all the slack in the rope and the rope is now tight to my harness."

Watch me!: Climber to belayer, "Heads up! Be attentive with the belay—there is a good chance I'm going to fall right here!"

Falling!: Climber to belayer, "I'm actually falling, go to your brake position and lock off the rope to catch my fall!" (A fall can happen so fast that the climber might not be able to shout this signal during a short fall, but it helps the belayer react more quickly, especially in situations where the belayer can't see the climber.)

ROCK!: Climber to belayer and others below, "I've dislodged a rock and it's now free-falling below me—watch out below!" (The equivalent signal to "fore!" in golf, "ROCK!" should also be yelled when the climber drops a piece of equipment.)

Belaying Technique

The best way to belay from the base of a climb (the most common way to belay a toprope situation, also called a slingshot or yo-yo setup) is to attach the rope and belay device directly to the belay loop on your harness with a locking carabiner. The rope then runs through the top anchor and back down to the climber. Your body weight serves as part of the anchor, and the added friction at the toprope anchor makes it relatively easy to catch a fall, hold a climber who is hanging on the rope, or lower a

Belaying Technique

The BUS (brake under slide) method of belaying on a toprope. Start by clipping the rope into the slot in the belay device closest to the spine side of the carabiner and orient the rope so that the brake side is down.

To take up rope, pull the rope up with your brake hand (palm down) as you simultaneously pull the rope down with the other hand . . .

climber back down. The belay device is right in front of you and easy to manipulate.

A slingshot toprope setup is essentially a redirected belay, because when the rope is run through the top anchor it adds more friction to the system, making for an easier catch on the belayer's end. Redirecting the rope through the anchor nearly doubles the force on the anchor (although friction reduces some of the force). The simplified physics work like this: When a 200-pound climber

Belaying Technique

. . . then brake the rope down under your belay device.

Take your non-brake hand and firmly grasp the rope directly under the belay device . . .

. . . then slide your brake hand up against that hand and repeat the process. This technique is easy to learn and maintains a firm brake position on the rope at all times. In a fall, remember that the brake position is down.

falls and hangs on the rope, he exerts at least 200 pounds of force on his side of the anchor. The belayer, holding the rope on the opposite side of the anchor, must also hold the climber's 200 pounds, so the anchor must absorb at least 400 pounds—200 pounds on each side of the anchor.

In situations where the climber far outweighs the belayer, or when the belayer is precariously perched in uneven terrain, the belayer should have a ground anchor.

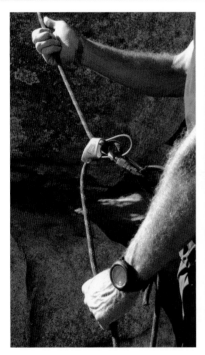

After you've mastered the BUS method, a more advanced technique is to brake under and switch the brake hand, alternating back and forth with either hand.

Two-Rope Toprope Setups

When rigging long topropes of more than half a single rope length, two ropes can be tied together using a double fisherman's knot or figure eight bend knot. With such a huge amount of rope out between the climber and the belayer, rope stretch is a major concern, especially if you are using dynamic ropes. Remember that even a short fall in a toprope situation will stretch a dynamic rope about 10 percent, so tighten up the rope when belaying someone just off the ground, or just above a ledge.

There are two methods that can be used to deal with the knot joining the two ropes. The simple solution, and also the best if there will not be a stance for the climber to stop at, avoids the knot pass altogether. With the knot joining the two ropes at the anchor, tie a figure eight loop and attach it to the climber's belay loop with two locking carabiners (gates opposed and reversed). When the climber reaches the anchor, the knot will be just above the belayer's device, so no knot pass is required.

Another solution is to use two belay devices. The climber ties in to the end of the rope as usual. The belayer anticipates the knot pass and has a second belay device clipped to his belay loop, at the ready. When the knot reaches the belayer, the belayer alerts the climber to find a good stance, then ties a backup knot (figure eight loop) on the brake hand side of the belay device. The belayer steps forward to create a bit of slack, then clips the rope into the second belay device on the climber's side of the knot, leaving the first belay device clipped in. If another person is available, he or she can assist the belayer simply by holding the rope with both hands under a little tension above the belay device as the belayer accomplishes this. When the climber reaches the anchor, the belayer lowers him until the knot is almost to the belay device, and the process is reversed: The climber takes a stance, the belayer unclips the second belay device (first double-checking that the first belay device is still clipped in and has the backup knot), then unties the backup knot and lowers the climber as normal. Knot-passing techniques are something that should be practiced with a qualified instructor.

The Ground Anchor

The worst accident I've had in thirty-five years of rock climbing happened when I was belaying in a toprope situation without a ground anchor. I was belaying from the base of the climb in a relaxed position about 15 feet out from the base of the cliff. Between the ledge I was belaying from and the cliff itself was a deep chimney. My partner was climbing on a toprope and suddenly fell while attempting an overhang about 50 feet above me. He swung wildly in the air. I easily caught the fall and locked off my belay device in the brake position, but I was pulled off my stance, swinging 15 feet straight into the wall like a pendulum. I braced for the impact with an outstretched leg and sustained a severely sprained ankle. A simple ground anchor would have prevented this accident. Belaying accidents are common, and in almost every case they have the same element: no ground anchor.

When should you use a ground anchor? If both the climber and belayer are roughly the same body weight and the terrain at the base of the cliff is flat, a ground anchor is unnecessary. But if the climber far outweighs the belayer, a ground anchor should always be considered. If the climb is vertical or

Above, This belayer is using a large block of rock for a ground anchor, ensuring she won't budge if the climber falls.

Left, Belayer anchored to a ground anchor with a clove hitch. The belayer is lowering a climber using a Grigri clipped to the harness belay loop.

overhanging, more force will be exerted by the falling climber than a fall on a low-angle climb. It is especially important to establish a ground anchor for the belayer in uneven terrain, particularly if the belay stance is perched high on top of boulders, or is some distance away from the base of the cliff.

A good system to rig a ground anchor is to start with the belayer tying in to the end of the rope. Not only does this "close" the rope system, but it allows the belayer to use the climbing rope to connect to a ground anchor with a clove hitch, which can be easily adjusted to suit the stance.

Natural anchors are obvious choices for ground anchors, like a sling or cordelette around a tree or a large block of rock. A single bomber cam or nut in a crack will also suffice.

If you are the belayer in a toprope scenario, anticipate that you will be pulled in a line directly to the toprope anchor master point, and anchor and brace yourself accordingly. Ideally, the ground anchor will be low and directly behind or beneath you or just slightly to the side. Remember your ABCs: anchor, belayer, climber. There should be a straight line between the anchor, the belayer, and the direction of pull created by the climber.

Safety Checks

Start by closing the system—this is an important habit to get into. Look at both ends of the climbing rope. Each end should either be tied into a climber's harness or have a stopper knot tied on the free end. This prevents a rope end from traveling through a belay or rappel device, thereby dropping the climber.

Tying a stopper knot.

In the toprope environment, it's critical to always close your rope system, either by tying in to the end of the rope, or tying a stopper knot like this.

Belayer Safety Checks

Check the belayer's harness, to make sure it is buckled properly. Check the figure eight follow-through knot, to make sure that it is (1) tied properly, and (2) threaded through the correct tie-in points at the front of the harness. Check the belayer's belay device, to make sure the rope is properly threaded through the device, and lastly, check the belayer's locking carabiner on the belay device, to make sure that it is locked. Check that the belayer is wearing her helmet.

Climber Safety Checks

Check the climber's harness, to make sure it is buckled properly. Check the climber's figure eight follow-through knot, to make sure that it is (1) tied properly, and (2) threaded through the correct tie-in points at the front of the harness. Check to ensure the climber is wearing his helmet.

Belaying from the Top

Top-Managed Sites

You may find yourself belaying from the top of the cliff for a variety of reasons. The cliff may only have access to the top, like a sea cliff, a river gorge, or a cliff with no practical access to the base. You may be teaching novices rappelling techniques. Whatever the reason, techniques used for belaying at the top of the cliff, based on the circumstances, will differ from those used at the base.

If the belayer is at the top of the cliff, belaying a climber who is ascending, lowering, or rappelling, the importance of a proper anchor is obvious. At the top of the cliff, the belayer can choose from a variety of belay methods, depending on the situation.

Belaying Off the Harness—
The Indirect Belay

The indirect belay method is when the belayer clips the rope and belay device into a locking carabiner attached to the belay loop on her harness. The belayer is "in the system," which means that if the climber falls, the belayer's body will absorb the force of the fall to some extent. I call it "indirect"

since the force generated in a fall does not necessarily go directly onto the anchor. For example, if the belayer takes a sitting stance and braces with her legs against a rock outcropping, and the climber falls, the belayer can absorb the force of the fall without transferring any load onto the anchor, accomplishing this by the stability of the stance aided by the friction of the rope running over the surface of the rock and at the belay device itself. When using the indirect belay, the anchor and stance are important because if the belayer gets pulled off-balance, or pulled sideways, she can easily lose control of the belay. The belayer should be anticipating the direction she will be pulled if a fall occurs, and position herself accordingly, tight to the anchor. The ABC acronym works in this situation: The belayer should be in a line between the anchor and the climber (anchor-belayer-climber).

While the indirect belay is commonly used by most recreational climbers, it is rarely used by trained, professional guides—for a number of reasons. One is that the belayer is trapped "in the system," and if a climber falls, the climber's weight is hanging directly off the belay loop of the belayer, making it difficult for her to even move. Once in

Belaying from the top with a redirected belay, Insomnia Crack, Suicide Rock, California.

this position, it is awkward for the belayer to hold the fallen climber, particularly if the stance is bad. Lowering the climber from the top of the cliff using an indirect belay can be difficult, if not dangerous, particularly if the cliff is steep and the climber far outweighs the belayer.

There was a fatal accident a few years ago at Joshua Tree when a belayer was lowering a climber from the top of a cliff using an indirect belay. The belayer had initially clipped into the top anchor with a short sling, but then unclipped from it, thinking that the rope itself (which he was tied into) was also clipped to the anchor. The climber being lowered far outweighed the belayer. The belayer lowered the climber with the rope clipped directly to an ATC attached to his harness's belay

Belaying with an indirect belay. The belayer is in a good seated stance, with the rope clipped to the master point into two locking carabiners with a figure eight loop. The ATC XP belay device is clipped to his belay loop with a locking carabiner. However, if the climber below falls, the belayer will have to absorb all the force and bear the full weight of the falling climber onto his harness. The braking position will be awkward, and since the belayer is slightly out of line from the direction of pull to the anchors, he will get pulled into that line. The belayer should simply position himself in line (anchor-belayer-climber, or ABC) to remedy this potential problem.

The old-school "pinch and slide technique" is commonly used as an indirect belaying technique when belaying from the top of a cliff. Start with the brake hand (the right hand in these photos) next to the belay device, with the left hand extended out.

Pull the rope in with the left hand and simultaneously pull rope out with the brake hand.

Move the brake hand back behind the braking plane (more than 90 degrees from the angle of the rope going to the climber) and pinch the rope above the brake hand with the left hand . . .

. . . then slide the brake hand down toward the belay device.

Move the left hand back to the extended position and repeat the process. The cardinal rule to remember with this method is to always keep the brake hand on the rope.

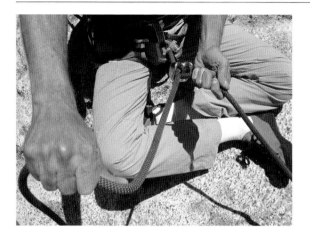

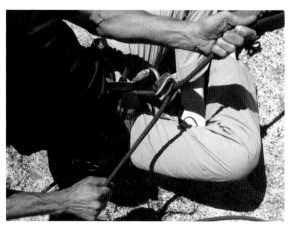

Another belay method for an indirect belay from the top of the cliff is a variation of the BUS (brake under slide) method, but instead of braking down, the brake position is up and back. The belayer's right hand is the brake hand in these photos. Starting with the brake hand palm down, the brake hand pulls the rope out as the left hand pulls rope in.

Next, the brake hand pulls the rope back into a brake position.

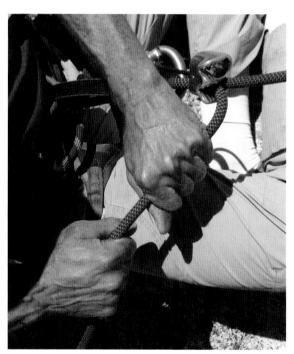

The left hand grasps the rope, palm down on the brake strand, just below the belay device.

The brake hand slides back toward the device without releasing its grip on the rope. The left hand extends again and grabs the non-brake side of the rope to repeat the process.

Climber Assistance Using an Indirect Belay

If you are belaying from the top and need to escape from the system and convert to a raising system to haul up a climber from below you, these would be the steps:

1. Tie off the belay device with a mule knot (Pass a bight of rope through your belay carbiner and tie the mule knot on the load strand above your belay device).

2. Tie a friction hitch (klemheist or prusik) on the load strand going to the climber.

3. Attach the friction hitch to a locking carabiner and tie a Munter/mule with the belayer's climbing rope (off the back side of the knot connecting the belayer to the anchor).

4. Tie a backup knot on the load strand and clip it to your anchor.

5. Build a 3:1 raising system using a prusik knot at the anchor as a ratchet, and another prusik knot on the load strand going to the climber.

loop. Everything was fine as the belayer lowered the climber on relatively flat terrain, until the climber stepped over the edge onto a steeper section of the wall and really put his weight onto the belay. The belayer could no longer maintain his position and was pulled off his stance. His rope was clipped into the anchor, but unfortunately there was 60 feet of slack in it, and the belayer went over the edge of the cliff until the anchored rope stopped his fall. Tragically, the climber who was being lowered hit the ground and was killed.

The indirect belay is also the worst method to use if the belayer needs to provide any assistance (like a raising system) to the climber below, since the belayer is trapped in the system and would need to perform a "belay escape" in order to get out of the system and convert it to a raise.

If this sound complicated, that's because it is! Complex self-rescue systems are beyond the scope of this book, but I detailed these steps to illustrate a point: An indirect belay is a poor choice for a top-managed toprope site. For more information on belay escapes, see *Self-Rescue*, 2nd edition (FalconGuides).

The Redirected Belay

This technique utilizes the additional friction generated by running the rope back through the anchor to help assist in catching a fall. Clip your belay device into your harness belay loop, then run the rope back through a locking carabiner at the anchor master point. If you're using a cordelette-style anchor setup, you can also redirect the rope through a locking carabiner clipped to the "shelf," which is defined as all the loops in the cordelette just above the master point knot. If your partner falls, you'll be pulled toward the anchor, so brace yourself for a pull in that direction. Because of the rope's friction through the redirect carabiner, you only have to hold about two-thirds of the force generated in the fall. The redirect nearly doubles the force on the anchor (just like in a toprope rig), so if you decide to use a redirected belay, the anchor should be bomber. The drawback to this technique, like the indirect belay, is that if any rescue or assistance skills are required, you'll have to perform a belay escape to rig any raising system.

The Direct Belay

The method preferred by most professional guides when belaying from the top of the cliff is the direct belay. In a direct belay the belay device is clipped directly to the anchor, and in the event of a fall, the anchor, not the belayer, bears the brunt of the fall and holds the climber's weight.

Using a standard belaying device, like an ATC, is not recommended for use in a direct belay, because

unless the device is positioned below your waist level, the braking position will be very awkward, and you will be in a weak and dangerous position to hold a fall. If the master point is above your waist level, the Munter hitch works well, since the braking position for maximum friction is when the two strands of rope are parallel to each other, with the brake position down below the carabiner, not above it.

The best way to set up a direct belay is to use

The redirected belay. If the climber below falls, the force on the belayer will be directly in line to where the rope is redirected through the anchor. The friction of the rope running over the redirect carabiner will absorb some of the force.

an assisted braking device, like a Grigri, attached directly to the master point on the anchor. The advantage of a Grigri or similar device is that in the event of a fall, the Grigri simply locks off, and the anchor holds the climber's weight. When using a Grigri in the direct belay mode, take care when the device is close to rock, as anything that presses against the handle (i.e., the rock) will release the

locking mechanism. Be sure to position the handle away from the rock.

Remember, a regular ATC or similar non-locking device is not recommended for use in a direct belay if the master point is at or above the belayer's waist level, as the braking position would be very awkward.

The direct belay. A Grigri is clipped directly to the master point.

Detail of a direct belay setup. The belayer is anchored with a clove hitch, and the Grigri is clipped directly to the anchor master point.

Climber Assistance Using a Direct Belay

I f you're belaying using the direct belay, and your climber needs assistance, a 3:1 raising system can be rigged in seconds, with no need to "escape the belay." The steps are as follows:

1. Tie a backup (overhand knot) on the brake hand side of the Grigri.

2. Tie a friction hitch (prusik or klemheist) on the load strand going to the climber.

3. Clip the brake strand into a carabiner attached to the friction hitch, untie the overhand backup knot, and you're ready to raise!

A Munter hitch or autolocking combo device (like the ATC Guide or Petzl Reverso) can also be used for a direct belay, but they are not as easily converted to a raising system as the Grigri. Again, for more information on rescue systems, check out *Self-Rescue,* 2nd edition (FalconGuides).

The Rope Direct Belay

If the belay anchor is initially built well back from the edge, and you want to belay from the edge to maintain a visual on the climber who's climbing up from below, you can use the climbing rope and a rope direct belay technique, which is essentially belaying off an extended master point. Attach your climbing rope to the master point on the anchor with a clove hitch on a locking carabiner, so you can adjust the length and position yourself just where you'd like at a stance near the edge where you can see the climber. Off the back side of the clove hitch, leave a little slack, then tie a figure eight loop and clip it into a separate locking carabiner to the master point. On this strand of rope, tie a figure eight loop and clip in your Grigri, at an ergonomic position slightly above you (toward the anchor) but not so far away that you can't reach the device and manipulate the handle if need be. I call this method "rope direct" because you are essentially belaying directly off the anchor, albeit extended whatever distance is required to position you at the edge. Using a device like a Grigri, you'll have the benefit of a quick and easy conversion to a raising system if required, and it's easy to lower someone on this setup by redirecting the brake strand on the Grigri (see "Lowering" in this chapter).

The rope direct belay rigging. This rigging technique allows you to position yourself away from the anchor and still use the direct belay technique, albeit on an extended master point. The belayer is on the left strand of rope, attached to the master point with a clove hitch to a locking carabiner. Off the back side of the clove hitch, the rope is clipped back to a separate carabiner with a figure eight loop. Off this strand, the Grigri is clipped to another figure eight loop. Here the distance is fairly close to the anchor, but this rigging technique is most useful for greater distances between the anchor and your desired belay stance, limited only by the length of available rope. The big advantage is visual contact with your climber in situations where the anchor is some distance back from the edge.

Lowering

Why would you lower someone down from the top of the cliff back to the base? Maybe you've just belayed the climber up, and she'd like to climb the route again, or an adjacent route; rather than convert the system to a rappel, it will be quicker to just lower her back down. Maybe the climber is a beginner and has never rappelled before, and you'd like to have better control in facilitating the descent. Whatever the reason, there are several lowering methods that are quick and easy to rig.

Lowering with a Grigri

My first choice is always to lower someone using a Grigri. Since it has a built-in autolock, there is no need to back it up with an autoblock. Petzl actually sells a carabiner, called the Freino, that has a

special gate on the side of the carabiner for the brake strand to be clipped into, to facilitate lowering. Without the special carabiner, you can redirect the brake strand back up through a separate carabiner clipped to the master point (or, on a cordelette anchor, up to the shelf). The big advantage of the Grigri is that once the rope is clipped in, you can use it for lowering (just remember to redirect the brake strand!) or belaying (as the climber climbs back up), and it's all set to rig a 3:1 hauling system if your climber needs some assistance on the way back up.

Lowering with a Munter Hitch

First make sure that you are anchored. A good way to do this is with a clove hitch tied on a locking carabiner clipped to the master point on the anchor. Flake the rope at your feet, so if there are

A Grigri in the lowering mode with the brake strand redirected using the Petzl Freino carabiner, which is specifically designed for this application.

A Grigri rigged for lowering with the brake strand redirected through a carabiner clipped to the master point.

any tangles, you can get to them. The clove hitch is adjustable, so you can fine-tune the length of your tie-in as required. If the stance at the anchor allows you to see down the cliff and watch the climber as you lower him, clip another locking carabiner (a large, pear-shaped carabiner works best) to the master point and tie a Munter hitch. Back it up with an autoblock clipped to a locking carabiner at your belay loop, and you're ready to lower your climber.

Tying the Munter Hitch

Hold a single strand of rope with both hands, thumbs pointing toward each other.

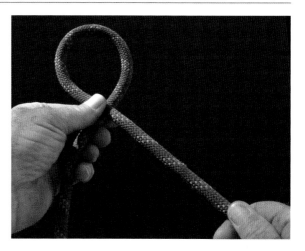

Cross the right hand strand in front of the left hand strand and hold the two strands where they cross with your left thumb and forefinger, then slide your right hand down about 6 inches.

Bring the right hand strand up and behind the loop you've created.

Clip a locking carabiner where the forefinger is shown here, below the top two strands.

The mule knot is used to tie off a Munter hitch. The great advantage of the Munter/mule combination is that it can be tied off and released when the rope is weighted and under tension, making it one of the key knot combinations for many rescue applications.

To tie off an ATC or similar tube device with a mule knot, first pass a bight of rope (on the brake hand side) through the belay carabiner and then tie the mule knot above your device on the load strand of rope going to the climber.

Tying a Mule Knot

When tying a mule, be aware that when the rope is under tension (holding a climber's weight), you'll need to keep a firm grip on the brake strand.

Keeping the load and brake strands parallel, form a loop on the brake strand by crossing it behind while still maintaining your grip with your brake hand.

With your non-brake hand, take a bight of rope and pass it through the loop you've created with the load strand in between the loop and the bight. Snug the mule knot up tight against the munter hitch.

Pull some slack, and finish with an overhand loop backup.

Using an Autoblock Knot as a Backup When Lowering

Whenever you are lowering a climber with a non-autolocking belay device, it's best to back up your brake hand with an autoblock knot clipped to a locking carabiner attached to your belay loop.

Some guides call the autoblock the "third hand," because if you take your brake hand off the rope when you're lowering or rappelling, the autoblock grabs the brake strand of your rope like your hand would. The autoblock adds an extra level of safety, especially when there are tangles in your rope that you need to untangle as you lower your climber or descend on a rappel.

If the stance at the anchor does not allow you to see down the cliff and watch the climber as you lower him, then you can rig the rope direct belay system to position yourself at the edge to maintain visual contact. As a guide, I always strive for visual contact with my client whenever belaying or lowering.

The belayer is ready to lower the climber with a Munter hitch on a locking carabiner clipped to the master point, backed up with an autoblock clipped to a locking carabiner attached to the belayer's belay loop.

Lowering with a Redirected Slot Device

To lower a climber with an ATC or similar device, clip the ATC to your harness and redirect the climber's strand back through the anchor at the master point. This adds friction and makes it easier to hold the climber's weight, but increases the load on the anchor—in fact, it nearly doubles it. Also, if the climber far outweighs the belayer, it can be very awkward and difficult to lower the climber, because the belayer is getting pulled into the anchor.

A better technique is to clip the ATC directly to the anchor master point and redirect the brake strand back through a locking carabiner at the master point (or, on a cordelette anchor, the shelf, which is all the loops in the cordelette just above the master point knot), to maintain the proper angle (for maximum friction) on the brake strand. Back it up with an autoblock attached to your belay loop with a locking carabiner. If you're using a combo device (like the ATC Guide or Petzl Reverso) and lowering the climber all the way to the base, and the plan is for them to climb back up, you can easily convert the device back to the autolocking belay mode once the climber reaches the ground and is ready to climb back up. If you're using a regular ATC or similar device, remember, *do not* use the device for a direct belay if the device is at your waist level or above, as the braking position would be weak, awkward, and dangerous. Rather, to belay the climber back up from the ground, switch the ATC to your belay loop and belay the climber back up with the climber's strand redirected through the master point, or position yourself for a rope direct belay with the ATC in an ergonomic braking position.

Black Diamond ATC XP device rigged with a redirect for lowering. The climber's end is coming out of the left side of the belay device, and the brake strand is redirected up through a carabiner clipped to the shelf.

Lowering with a Munter hitch and an autoblock. The belayer is holding an autoblock backup that's clipped with a locking carabiner to his belay loop.

Rappelling

The descent from the top of a toproping crag usually entails a walk-off trail or a Class 3 descent off the side or back of the cliff, but in most situations, once you've set up a toprope anchor and want to begin climbing, it will be most expedient to rappel straight down to the base. Making the transition safely from the top of the cliff to a rappel is more complicated when you have a toprope setup rigged with an extension rope, since you have to reach the climbing rope below the edge. Doing this safely is detailed in chapter 8 (the Joshua Tree System and the Fox System).

Many cliffs also have fixed anchors for rappelling. These are typically trees (often a single, bombproof tree with slings and rappel rings) or, more commonly, a two-bolt anchor rigged with metal rings through which you can thread your rope. Your rappel anchor should be redundant. Even if it's just a single, big pine tree, inspect the slings and rings for redundancy. The rigging should have two separate slings around the tree and two rings through which you can thread your rope.

To rappel with an ATC or similar tube device, thread a bight of both strands of rope through the device and clip them in to a locking carabiner attached to your belay loop. Keep the cable on the ATC clipped in to the carabiner while you do this, so you won't drop the device. As you thread the ropes through your device, position the brake strands down, toward your feet. This will allow the rope to feed smoothly through the device with

Two-bolt rappel anchor with rings.

Rappel anchor with two slings and two rings.

Proper rappelling stance for good stability, with a slightly crouched position and wide base for the feet, looking over one shoulder to watch where she's going.

no twists. If you have a device with different friction options, like the ATC XP, decide if you want more or less friction. (With the ATC XP, placing the teeth side down on the braking side will give you the most friction, non-teeth side down, less friction.) How much friction you want depends on these variables: the diameter of the rope, the slickness of the rope's sheath, your body weight, and the angle of the rock face you're rappelling down.

For a steep rappel I prefer to hold the ropes with both hands below the device in the braking position, with the ropes going down between my legs. For less steep rappels, I hold the ropes off to my right side, since I'm right-handed, and grab the ropes with my right hand as my brake hand at my hip.

Black Diamond ATC XP rigged for a double-rope rappel in high-friction mode.

Rappelling Safeguards: Preventing Rappel Accidents

Although rappelling is a simple technique, statistically a high percentage of rappelling accidents end in a fatality. Why is this? Perhaps rappelling is so rudimentary that the fine points of safety are sometimes overlooked. Analyzing rappelling accidents tells us what can go wrong. Let's take a look at two scenarios in some detail.

SCENARIO 1: RAPPELLING OFF ONE OR BOTH ENDS OF THE ROPE

Believe it or not, this happens with some regularity, and almost every year there are several fatal rappelling accidents in America where someone has simply rappelled off the ends of a rope. Usually it happens when the ends are uneven on a doubled rope rappel. When the short end passes through the rappelling device, only one strand of the doubled rope remains in the device, and the climber's body weight will rapidly pull the rope through the rappel anchor, quickly dispatching the climber to the ground. A simple solution is to tie knots separately in both ends of the rope using stopper knots. It's a simple solution, and a key safety habit in the single-pitch environment, no matter what you're using the rope for.

SCENARIO 2: NOT CLIPPING BOTH STRANDS OF THE ROPE INTO THE CARABINER

This is an easy mistake to make if you're not alert and double-checking your system. If you thread both strands of rope through your rappel device, but only clip one strand into your locking carabiner, when you lean back and weight the rope, you'll descend as rapidly as in the first scenario, and with equally injurious or fatal results. A good safety habit is to first clip in with a sling to the rappel anchor, rig your rappel device, then weight the rappel system and double-check everything *before* unclipping the sling. Always go through a mental checklist before rappelling: ABC. A is the rappel anchor. Take

a look at the anchor, slings, chains, etc., and make sure the rappel rope is threaded properly through the anchor. The anchor should be redundant all the way to the point where your rope is threaded through the anchor. What this means is that you should not rely on a single piece of gear in your anchor system, whether it is a single cord, sling, or rappel ring. B is for buckles on your harness—double-check to make sure they are buckled properly and doubled back appropriately. C is for carabiner. Make sure the locking carabiner that attaches your rappel device to your harness is being loaded properly on the long axis—and check to make sure that it is locked!

Rappel Belays

If you're teaching a beginner and they're rappelling for the first time, it's best to belay them on a separate rope (see "Teaching Rappelling" in chapter 10). Another technique to back up somebody on rappel is called the fireman's belay. This is done by having someone down below attentively holding both strands of the rappel rope (in a doubled rope rappel). When this person pulls down on the ropes and applies tension, the rappeller will stop on a dime—they cannot move down the rope when it is under tension.

Rappel Backups

In the old days the most common method for a rappel backup was using a prusik knot on the ropes *above* the rappel device, connected to the harness with a sling. The non-brake hand would cup the prusik knot and hold it in a loosened position during the rappel, allowing it to slide down the rope. Letting go of the knot allowed it to slide up and grab onto the ropes, stopping the rappel. There are two drawbacks with this method. One is that for the prusik to lock off, it must hold all the rappeller's weight. The second is that once it is weighted, the rappeller must remove all his body weight from the prusik knot in order for it to be released, not an easy task if you're on a free-hanging rappel. In essence, to take your weight off the prusik, you might need the skills to perform a mini self-rescue.

The modern rappel backup utilizes the autoblock knot, rigged *below* the rappel device. There are two distinct advantages with this method. One is that for the autoblock knot to grab, it only needs to hold a very small percentage of the rappeller's weight, since it is on the braking side of the device, and the device itself is holding most of the weight and providing most of the friction. It is essentially like your brake hand squeezing and gripping the rope, and for that reason some instructors refer to

it as the "third hand," like an angel grabbing your rope and averting a catastrophe, if for some reason you've lost control of the brake. The second big advantage of the autoblock method is that it is releasable under tension (i.e., when you've weighted it and it's grabbing onto the rope). As you rappel down, you simply take your thumb and forefinger, forming a circle (like the OK sign), and push the autoblock down as you go, allowing the rope to freely slide through the knot. When you let go, the autoblock knot rides up and grabs onto the rope, like your brake hand squeezing the rope. To release the autoblock, even with your weight on it, is as

Black Diamond ATC XP rigged for rappelling with a three-wrap autoblock backup clipped to the leg loop with a locking carabiner.

Another view of how to rig an autoblock backup, here using a Black Diamond ATC rappel device and a three-wrap autoblock tied with 6 mm nylon cord attached to the leg loop with a locking carabiner.

simple as sliding it back down and holding it in the "open" position with your fingers. It's a beautiful thing, and easy to rig.

The disadvantage of clipping the autoblock to your leg loop is that if for some reason you were to go unconscious and flip upside down, the autoblock could ride up and come in contact with your rappel device, which would prevent it from grabbing, much like sliding it down and keeping it "open" with your fingers. In recent years professional guides have developed a method to safeguard against this, simply by extending the rappel device with a sling attached to the harness, and rigging the autoblock clipped into the belay loop. I like to rig a double-length sewn nylon sling threaded through both points at the front of my harness (where your rope tie-in goes through) and tied with an overhand knot, to gain redundancy at the sling. I prefer to use a fat nylon sling over a thin Spectra or Dyneema sling for this application because nylon has a higher melting point. If the rappel rope is running across the sling, it could potentially create some heat due to the friction, which could damage the sling and reduce its breaking strength in later applications.

Adam Fox, Discipline Coordinator of the AMGA's Single Pitch Instructor program, demonstrates proper use of an extended rappel device with autoblock backup. A double-length nylon runner is threaded through the harness tie-in points and tied with an overhand knot for redundancy. The rappel device is the Black Diamond ATC Guide in the rappel mode. The autoblock knot is clipped to a locking carabiner attached to the belay loop.

In a pinch the Munter hitch can be used for rappelling, although it will put some kinks in your rope. Position the gate of the carabiner opposite the braking side of the Munter hitch, so there is no chance the movement of the rope can unscrew or open the gate.

CHAPTER EIGHT

Advanced Toprope Anchor Rigging Systems

The Joshua Tree System

A typical day for a rock climbing instructor at Joshua Tree National Park begins early in the morning. Clients will soon be arriving, and topropes must be set up in advance to secure a spot to begin the day's climbing. Joshua Tree is a vast area, with hundreds of crags to choose from, and the setups can be time-consuming and gear intensive, because most anchors require gear placements set well back from the cliff edge, and bolted anchors are a rarity. Out of necessity guides at Joshua Tree developed a system to rig toprope anchors that is both efficient and redundant, using a length of low-stretch rigging rope. I call it the Joshua Tree System.

To rig the Joshua Tree System, visualize a V configuration, with two separate sets of anchors on the top of the V and the point, or bottom, of the V being the toprope master point over the edge of the cliff. Ideally, the angle of the V should be as narrow as possible—at least less than 90 degrees. Once

you have determined where the climb is and where you want your master point, picture the V in your mind and begin to set your anchors. If using natural anchors it could be as simple as two trees. For simplicity let's say we have two anchors: anchor A and anchor B. Start by attaching one end of your rigging rope to anchor A. This can be done either by using a sling or cordelette and a locking carabiner to a figure eight loop, or by tying the rope directly around the tree. (I prefer the re-threaded bowline for tying a rope to a tree.)

Now, for safety as you approach the cliff edge, protect yourself by taking a prusik cord (6 mm-diameter soft nylon, 4 feet 6 inches long, tied into a loop with a double fisherman's knot) and attaching it to your rigging rope with a prusik or klemheist knot. Take a single-length sling and girth-hitch it to the front of your harness by threading it through the same two points your rope tie-in goes through, then attach the sling to your prusik cord with a locking carabineer. A nylon sling is better for this

A man tries rock climbing for the first time on a toprope at the South Slabs at Garden of the Gods, Colorado.
STEWART M. GREEN

application because nylon has some stretch, whereas Spectra or Dyneema are static (like a wire cable) and have no stretch. Now you can slide the prusik knot up and down the rigging rope to safeguard

yourself as you work near the edge. Tie a BHK (see photos) so that your master point dangles just over the lip of the cliff edge, positioned directly above your chosen climb. Attach your climbing rope with

Tying the BHK "Big Honking Knot"

Start by taking a doubled bight about 4 feet long.

Gather all four strands . . .

carabiners (either two opposed and reversed locking, or three opposed and reversed ovals) and run the rope back to anchor B, attaching it with a clove hitch to a locking carabiner. This will allow you to adjust the tension and fine-tune the equalization.

Continued on Page 150

. . . then tie an overhand loop on all four strands.

For extra safety, I like to take the single loop and hitch it all the way back around the body of the two-loop knot.

Overview of the Joshua Tree System. The right "leg" of the extension rope is attached with a figure eight loop to a locking carabiner clipped to a master point on a three-piece anchor pre-equalized with a cordelette. The left leg of the extension rope goes to a two-piece anchor pre-equalized with another cordelette, attached with a clove hitch on a locking carabiner for adjustment of the extension rope. A BHK is tied for the master point, with two opposed and reversed locking carabiners ready for the climbing rope.

Above, Close-up of the master point on the Joshua Tree System using a BHK and three steel oval carabiners with the gates opposed and reversed.

Right, Sierra Club leader Dan Richter demonstrates proper use of a friction knot for safety while rigging a toprope. He's using a klemheist knot attached to a sling connected to his harness, rigged on one leg of his toprope extension rope.

Toprope all day long with your extension rope rubbing on a sharp edge . . .

In the Joshua Tree System we call the rigging rope an "extension" rope or "extendo" rope. The two separate strands of rope that run from the master point to anchors A and B are the "legs" of the extension rope.

Take care to make sure the extension rope is not resting over sharp edges at the lip of the cliff. This setup is an "unmonitored" anchor system, which means that once rigged, you'll be at the base and not able to watch what is happening at the anchor—like the extension rope abrading over an edge, so take special care to prevent this by padding the edge (a pack or rope bag will work) or, better yet, use commercially made edge protectors.

If you learn to tie double loop knots like the

. . . and you'll end up with a seriously abraded rope like this one.

A commercially made edge protector, like this one sold by Petzl, is a wise investment.

Take two strands of the bight and wrap them around the standing part, then poke them through the loop.

Take a bight of rope and cross it back over itself, forming a loop.

To finish, take the loop at the very end of the bight and fold it down and around the entire knot you've just formed.

double loop figure eight and double loop bowline, along with the in-line figure eight, you'll be able to eliminate many slings and cordelettes from your anchor system and become more efficient in your rigging. For example, when using the Joshua Tree System, I often start with two bomber pieces at the end of one leg on my extension rope, then equalize them with a double loop knot, thus eliminating the need for slings or cordelettes. As I move toward the edge and perhaps find more anchor placements, I use the in-line eight to equalize these pieces to the system. The double loop knots and in-line eight are illustrated here for those who wish to become master riggers!

The double loop figure eight is a great knot to use to equalize two gear placements. You can manipulate the knot by loosening one strand and feeding it through the body of the knot, shortening one loop, which makes the other loop larger.

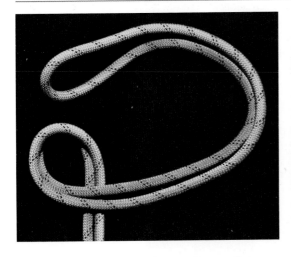

Take a bight of rope and cross it over the standing part.

Thread the bight through the loop you've just formed.

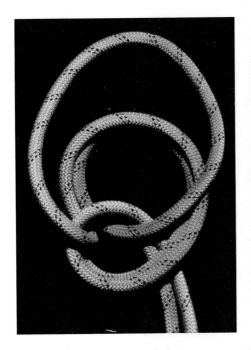

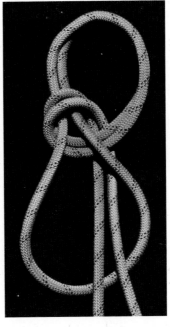

Configure the end of the bight in a loop above the rest of the knot.

Flip the loop down like a hinge behind the rest of the knot.

Pull on the two loops until the end of the bight tightens at the base of the knot.

The two loops can be adjusted by feeding one strand into the body of the knot, which alternately shortens one loop and lengthens the other.

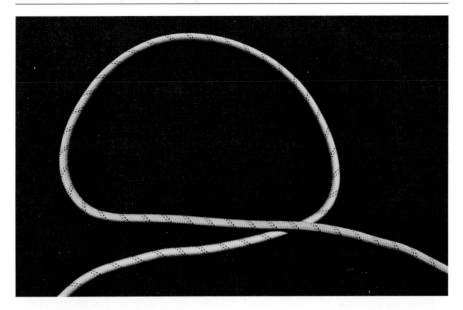

This knot, like the clove hitch, can be used with the extension rope to attach to a series of anchors in a line. It takes some practice to master this knot, but after you do you may find it easier to use than a clove hitch. Cross the strands to form a simple loop.

Cross a bight over the single strand.

Cross the bight under the strand.

Thread the bight back through the loop you've just formed.

Finished in-line figure eight.

When rigging the Joshua Tree System, the double loop eight is another good knot to use for the master point on the extension rope. Technically, it is not as redundant as the BHK, but it presents a cleaner profile (it doesn't have the extra loop to deal with) and gives you a two loop master point, which has garnered it favor with rescue teams and professional guides for critical applications.

Making the Transition from Rigging to Rappelling

If you decide to rappel to the base, you will need to transition from your extension rope to your rappel rope. Slide your prusik safety knot down one leg of the extension rope until you approach the edge. Before you get to the edge, pull up your doubled rappel rope, rig your rappel device, and back it up with an autoblock. The sling that goes to the prusik should be long enough so that as you make the

Here a prusik is tied around one leg of the extension rope, attached with a locking carabiner to the silver sling that's girth hitched around the climber's belay loop. Before they descended to this position, their rappel device (an ATC) was attached and backed-up with an autoblock tied around the brake strands of the rappel rope, attached with a locking carabiner to the climber's leg loop. Notice that the silver sling/orange prusik cord is long enough so that the climber's weight is on the ATC and autoblock combination before the sling comes tight.

transition to weight your rappel/autoblock setup, the sling does not tighten first. If you've rigged your rappel device to your belay loop, and the autoblock is at your leg loop, a single sling should suffice. However, if you've extended your rappel device away from your harness with a sling and rigged your autoblock at your belay loop, you'll need a double-length sling to your prusik to allow you enough length to weight your rappel/autoblock setup before the sling to your prusik tightens.

A close-up view demonstrating a pre-rigged rappel setup. While at the top of the cliff the climber would first girth-hitch the yellow sling to their harness, then attach it with a locking carabiner to the orange prusik on one leg of the extension rope. They would then pull up the extension rope and pre-rig their ATC rappel device on the rappel rope and back it up with a three-wrap autoblock tied below the ATC on the braking strands and attach it to their belay loop with a locking carabiner. To descend to this position they would slide the prusik down the rope for protection. Now, to embark on the rappel, they simply unclip from the yellow sling, de-rig the prusik, and they're good to go.

The Fox System

Developed by Adam Fox, founder of Fox Mountain Guides, the Fox System was conceived as an efficient rigging system for professional guides that addresses the needs for instructor safety, top-managed scenarios, and easy conversion to a bottom-managed site.

The rigging sounds complicated, but after you do it a few times it will seem relatively simple. You'll need a length of approximately 120 feet of static or low-stretch rope to rig the Fox System in most situations.

Start by building two anchor systems similar to how you would with the Joshua Tree System, keeping in mind that a narrow-angle V configuration (or at least less than 90 degrees) is your goal, because you will be creating a high master point about 10 feet back from the edge to allow yourself a nice "desktop" from which to work. Tie a figure eight loop on one end of your static rigging line and clip it in to the anchor farthest away from the edge. Create a V running from this anchor to your high master point, then back to your next anchor. Tie a BHK at the high master point. Take the other end

Rappelling on an instructor tether using a Grigri.

of the rigging rope and tie a stopper knot in the end. Toss the end so it hangs down about 10 feet below the edge, then attach it to the high master point with a figure eight loop to two opposed and reversed locking carabiners. This is your instructor tether, which you can clip into with your Grigri or ABD. You are now set up for a top-managed scenario, like a belayed rappel, working off the high master point.

It's easy to convert to a base-managed site and set up a toprope, because you can now safely approach the cliff edge via your tether for further rigging. This is particularly useful if the top is slanting or angled down to an exposed edge. Take the rope off the back side of your instructor tether from the high master point and run it over the edge, tie a BHK, then go back to the high master point and attach the rope with a clove hitch to another locking carabiner at the high master point. You now have a new, extended master point over the edge ready for your toprope climbing rope.

Using a Grigri on an instructor tether (with a backup knot on the brake side), this instructor is lowering a climber by using a Munter hitch at the high master point. An autoblock backup is rigged on the brake strand side, attached to his leg loop with a locking carabiner.

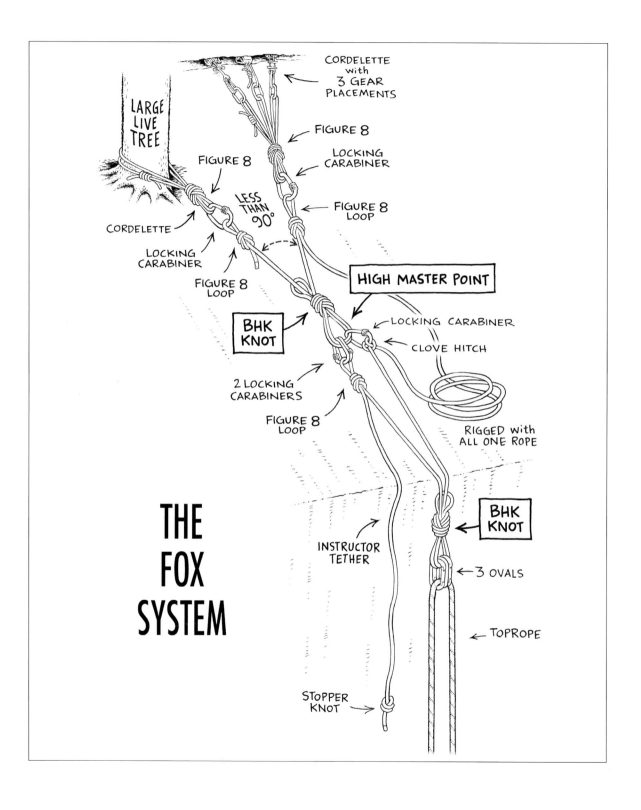

CORDELETTE with 3 GEAR PLACEMENTS

LARGE LIVE TREE

FIGURE 8

LOCKING CARABINER

FIGURE 8

LESS THAN 90°

FIGURE 8 LOOP

CORDELETTE

LOCKING CARABINER

FIGURE 8 LOOP

HIGH MASTER POINT

LOCKING CARABINER

CLOVE HITCH

BHK KNOT

2 LOCKING CARABINERS

FIGURE 8 LOOP

RIGGED with ALL ONE ROPE

BHK KNOT

INSTRUCTOR TETHER

3 OVALS

TOPROPE

THE FOX SYSTEM

STOPPER KNOT

Guide Massey Teel using a Grigri on an instructor tether as a safety while rigging the Fox System. Note the backup knot tied on the rope below the Grigri.

Left, the Fox System. The anchors could be any combination of gear or natural anchors. With gear anchors, two placements at the end of each leg of the high master point "V" is a good minimum. The clove hitch allows easy adjustment of the toprope "V," but I prefer to tie a figure eight loop here instead, lowering the "V" over the edge with a few carabiners as ballast to find the equalized point, then pulling it up to tie the BHK last.

Making the transition when rappelling with a Grigri on an instructor tether. The rappel device is pre-rigged—extended on a doubled nylon sling and backed up with an autoblock knot attached with a locking carabiner to his belay loop. Once the climber descends on the tether below the master point and weights his pre-rigged rappel system, he can double-check everything before unclipping the Grigri.

Making the Transition from Rigging to Rappelling

To rappel back to the base, use your instructor tether to facilitate a safe, easy transition to a pre-rigged rappel. Simply pull up your doubled rappel rope, rig your rappel device, back it up with an autoblock, then rappel on your instructor tether with your Grigri until you're tight to your pre-rigged rappel setup. Double-check your rappel device and make sure your autoblock is grabbing, then unclip from your Grigri and you're ready to rappel on your climbing rope.

Rappelling on an instructor tether to a pre-rigged rappel for a safe transition. The tether is very useful in situations like this where the master point has been extended a considerable distance down steep and exposed terrain.

Basic Assistance and Rescue Skills

Assistance from the Base

In over twenty-five years of professionally guiding thousands of clients in toprope situations, I've only had a few instances where I actually had to go up on the rock and bring a climber down—all of them being young kids who were overcome by fear and mentally lost control, afraid to lean back and weight the rope so they could be lowered back down. Having the knowledge and skills to go up the rope and bring a climber down is important in case you ever have to assist an injured climber, even in a toprope situation.

I call this technique the "climber pickoff," and it is essentially the same technique used by the belayer to rescue a fallen lead climber who is injured and can't be lowered. The difference in a toprope situation is that you're dealing with a bomber anchor, not just the one piece of gear that held the leader's fall.

The climber pickoff is most easily accomplished with an ABD, like a Grigri, and I highly recommend using a Grigri for belaying from both the base and top of the cliff, as it streamlines and facilitates all the basic rescue techniques described here. As a guide I always use one, since it's the right tool for the job and worth every extra ounce that it weighs over a traditional belay device. I'd also recommend first learning the climber pickoff—and the 3:1 raising system described next—with a Grigri before trying it without one. If you're interested in learning more advanced self-rescue techniques, I highly recommend reading *Self-Rescue,* 2nd edition, by David Fasulo (FalconGuides).

The climber pickoff utilizes a counterbalance ascension and rappel technique, and requires minimal equipment. Basically you ascend the rope to the climber, then rappel down with them.

All you need is the following equipment:

1 double-length (48-inch) sling

1 locking carabiner

1 prusik cord (5 mm or 6 mm soft nylon cord, 4.5 feet long, tied into a sling with a double fisherman's knot.)

If you are already belaying with a Grigri, here are the steps:

1. Start by tying a backup knot (overhand loop) on the brake strand side of the Grigri.
2. Tie a friction hitch (klemheist or prusik) with your prusik cord on the load strand going up to the climber, and attach your double-length sling to it with a locking carabiner.

Counterbalance rappel using a Grigri after "picking off"
a climber from the cliff.

3. Ascend the rope by sliding the friction hitch up, so that when you put your foot in the sling your knee is bent at a 90-degree angle. You can tie a knot in the sling to shorten it as needed. Stand up in the sling, and as you straighten your leg, simultaneously pull the slack through the Grigri (pulling straight up on the brake strand) and hang in your harness off the Grigri. Alternate standing up in the sling, then hanging in your harness, tight to the Grigri. About every 10 feet or so, tie a backup knot (overhand loop) on the brake strand side of the Grigri.

4. When you reach the climber, transfer the friction hitch from your side of the rope onto the rope above the climber you're assisting. Take the double-length sling and thread it (basket style) through your belay loop, and clip both ends of the sling to the locking carabiner attached to the friction hitch. Where you position the friction hitch will affect where the assisted climber will be positioned. If the friction hitch is as high as you can slide it, the climber will remain at that position as you both rappel. If you position the friction hitch (klemheist or prusik) just above the knot, the climber will move up and slightly above you before you both descend.

5. Rappel with the Grigri, untying the backup knots as you descend.

If you are taking over someone else's belay, the sequence would be as follows:

1. Tie a backup knot (overhand loop) on the brake strand side of the belayer's belay device.
2. Clip your Grigri onto the rope between the backup knot and the belayer's belay device.

Left, Basic assistance skills will allow you to assist your partner if needed.

3. Tie a friction hitch (prusik or klemheist) on the load strand (going up to the climber) of the belayer's rope.

4. Thread (basket style) the double-length sling through the belayer's belay loop and attach it to the friction hitch with a locking carabiner.

5. Have the belayer give slack at his belay device—the tension will now be transferred to the friction hitch, with the belayer essentially becoming a ground anchor; the belayer then can unclip and remove his belay device.

6. Transfer the weight of the hanging climber from the belayer to your Grigri, by taking up all the slack in the rope and pulling upward on the brake strand side of the Grigri, using your body weight as the anchor.

7. Unclip one end of the sling from the locking carabiner at the friction hitch.

8. Ascend the rope by sliding the friction hitch up, so that when you put your foot in the sling your knee is bent at a 90-degree angle. You can tie a knot in the sling to shorten it as needed. Stand up in the sling, and as you straighten your leg, simultaneously pull the slack through the Grigri (pulling straight up on the brake strand) and hang in your harness off the Grigri. Alternate standing up in the sling, then hanging in your harness, tight to the Grigri. About every 10 feet or so, tie a backup knot (overhand loop) on the brake strand side of the Grigri.

9. When you reach the climber, transfer the friction hitch from your side of the rope onto the rope above the climber you're assisting. Take the double-length sling and thread it (basket style) through your belay loop, and clip both ends of the sling to the locking carabiner attached to the friction hitch. Where you position the friction hitch will affect where the climber you are bringing down will be positioned. If the friction hitch is as high as you can slide it, the climber will remain at that position as you both rappel. If you position the friction hitch (klemheist or prusik) just above the knot, the climber will move up and slightly above you before you both descend.

10. Rappel with the Grigri, untying the backup knots as you descend.

Assistance from the Top

Coaching

The best and easiest way to assist a climber who's climbing up to you from below is simply to position your belay stance where you'll be able to watch them. By having visual contact you'll be able to manage the belay more effectively, taking in slack in synch with the movement of the climber. Giving advice to a climber who encounters a challenging section may prove ineffective if you can't actually see them.

Vector Pull

If someone just physically can't do a move or is too tired to climb up a tough crux section, some assistance from the belayer may be enough to get them over the impasse. A simple method is the vector pull.

Imagine a rope strung tight across a chasm, anchored on both ends, rigged for a climber to clip in with a pulley and slide across. This is known as a Tyrolean traverse. If the climber weighs 200 pounds and he is hanging from the middle of the rope, with an angle slightly less than 180 degrees, the force at each anchor is roughly 1,000 pounds. As the angle approaches 180 degrees, the force on the anchor points increases even more. Less angle, less force. For example, when the angle is relatively narrow (22 degrees or less) the 200 pound climber would be weighting each anchor with 100 pounds. With a rope tight (180-degree angle), by reaching down and pulling perpendicular to the line of the rope, a surprising amount of force can be generated just by creating an angle slightly less than 180 degrees. Your hand, pulling on the rope at a right angle, is like the climber hanging in the middle of the Tyrolean traverse who is generating 10 times his bodyweight at the anchor points. This is often enough to boost someone past a move, especially if they are able to assist by climbing themselves.

3:1 Raising System

One reason to use the direct belay technique with an assisted braking device when belaying from the top of the cliff is that it is easily converted to a 3:1 raising system (aka the Z system) in a matter of seconds. As a climbing guide the direct belay is my first choice, providing the anchor is bomber, because it allows me to anticipate and prepare for any eventuality, like a quick lowering or raising of the climber. I use my Grigri, clipped directly to the master point or extended master point (using the climbing rope). To set up a 3:1 raise, follow these steps:

1. Tie a backup knot (overhand loop) on the brake strand side of the Grigri. Now I'm "hands free" and can take my brake hand off the rope.
2. Tie a friction hitch (prusik or klemheist) on the load strand going down to the climber.
3. Clip the brake strand side of the rope (from the Grigri) to a locking carabiner clipped to the friction hitch. Now untie the backup knot and pull up on the brake strand side of the rope. Pulling 3 feet on your end raises the load 1 foot. Friction is your enemy when raising with a 3:1. If the rope going to the climber is in contact with a large surface area of rock, the raise will be correspondingly more difficult. A pulley at the friction hitch carabiner reduces friction and makes it easier to pull. Remember, this technique is for assisting a climber, helping them get past a tough spot, not to haul up a severely injured or unconscious climber.
4. When the friction hitch is all the way to the Grigri, reset the friction hitch by sliding it back down toward the climber. The Grigri's built-in ratchet will lock off and hold the load as you do this. Then continue the raise.

3:1 Assisted Raise

For this method the climber must be close enough that you can throw her a bight of rope. The climber clips the rope into her harness to assist in the raise. Using this system allows both the climber and rescuer to work together, and makes it much easier for the rescuer to raise the climber.

If you are the belayer/rescuer, the steps are as follows:

1. Tie a backup knot (overhand loop) on the brake strand side of your Grigri (or self-locking belay device).
2. Toss a bight of rope down to the climber and have her clip it in to her belay loop with a locking carabiner.
3. Identify which strand the climber should pull on by shaking it.
4. Untie the backup knot.
5. The climber pulls down as you pull up on the brake strand side of the rope. Warn the climber to watch her hands so they are not pinched in the carabiner as you pull.

A 3:1 assisted raise. With the climber also pulling, you get a tremendous mechancial advantage, making it far easier to raise someone than with a 3:1 raise.

CHAPTER TEN

Teaching Rock Climbing in a Toprope Environment

The effective instructor is not someone who simply demonstrates a wealth of knowledge and expertise. It is someone who is able to convey information about what they know in a way that others can readily comprehend, understand, remember, and then go out and use themselves.

When teaching a figure eight follow-through knot to a group of six novices, this is what I've found typically happens: About half the group gets it right the first time, two people get it right after a few tries, and one person just can't get it right even after multiple tries. Why is this? People have differing learning styles, and it is usually not a question of intelligence, but rather a problem with the way the information is being presented that does not suit their particular learning style. Often, taking a different approach with the presentation of the information will help in comprehension and retention.

Learning Styles

The three main learning styles I've encountered as an instructor are visual, auditory (verbal), and kinesthetic. Although most of us are some combination of different learning styles, we are usually predominate in one.

The visual learner picks up information most effectively by reading the written word and viewing photos or illustrations. They need to see it to learn it. This group represents the highest percentage of the population (roughly 65 percent), and they learn most effectively from written communication. The visual learner thinks in pictures and words. They prefer their information presented in a written format as opposed to the spoken word, and usually prefer to take detailed notes when presented with verbal information. They can have difficulty with spoken directions. For example, a verbal description of how to get to some place is likely ineffective to them, but a written description along with a map would prove useful. For this group charts, diagrams, graphs, and visual schematics are highly effective. When teaching a knot to this group, a verbal description is of little help, but presenting the sequence of tying the knot like a schematic diagram, with step 1, step 2, and so forth, may prove more successful.

The auditory, or verbal, learner represents

Jose Maestas toproping a hard route on the Ripple Wall at Red Rock Canyon Open Space, Colorado.

Climbing class toproping at Suicide Rock, California.
TONY GRICE

another large segment of the population (around 30 percent) and learns most effectively from the spoken word. They need to hear it to learn it. This group is comprised of the most sophisticated speakers, and they relate most effectively to spoken words. They are good listeners. They will listen attentively to a verbal presentation and take notes afterward. They benefit from hearing lectures and participating in group discussions. They prefer their information presented in a verbal format, and for them information is not tangible unless it is spoken. They can have difficulty with written directions.

Another, much smaller percentage of people are kinesthetic learners, who learn by doing, by getting the feel and tactile sensation of performing the steps required to learn a task. They usually are gifted athletes, and can learn a knot just by seeing it tied, then tying it once or twice. I've worked with a number of the most elite Navy Seals (Seal Team 6), and they are mostly kinesthetic learners, able to pick up abstract concepts, like tying a knot, very quickly. The kinesthetic learner prefers hands-on learning, but can appear slow if information is not presented to them in a style that suits their learning method.

Many people learn most effectively by watching, doing, and reflecting on a particular technique.

Around 450 BC the great Chinese philosopher Confucius said: "Tell me and I will forget; show me and I may remember; involve me and I will understand." Various research studies point to the fact that people remember best by watching a demonstration, having a discussion, practicing the skill, then teaching it to others. Military trainers use the EDIP principal (explain, demonstrate, imitate, practice).

When teaching climbing techniques, I always try to present the topic in a way that most broadly targets all the differing learning styles. My approach is simple:

1. Tell
2. Show
3. Do

Learning knots at Joshua Tree National Park, California.

Using this approach, here is an example of how I would teach an abstract concept, such as a complicated knot:

1. Tell. A verbal explanation targets the verbal or auditory learning style, so I verbally describe the steps to tie the knot.
2. Show. I demonstrate the knot. Facing in the same direction (the mirror image) as the person you're teaching is helpful. This targets the visual learning style.
3. Do. I have the person I'm teaching practice tying the knot. This benefits the kinesthetic learner.

This is the basic approach, although there are additional teaching methods that will help in memory retention and learning, namely imagery and mnemonic devices. An example of using imagery when teaching the bowline knot: "The snake comes up through the hole, around the tree, and back down through the hole." Attaching a verbal image of an animal or thing is one of the most effective ways to remember an abstract concept. I've found this approach very effective for teaching the figure eight follow-through to large groups of ten-year-old Boy Scouts: "Make a face with the rope. OK, if this is the face, then where is the neck? OK, this is the neck, and this is the face. Take the rope and choke it behind the neck, then poke it into the face."

Mnemonic devices are another form of memory aid. The most common one is the acronym. The military is big on acronyms, like IED (improvised explosive device), SOTG (Special Operations Training Group), etc. In teaching climbing, some common acronyms are ABC (anchor, belayer, climber), BARCK (buckle, anchor, rope, carabiner, knot), and RENE (Redundancy, Equalization, and No Extension).

To most effectively teach climbing techniques, take an approach that presents the information in a broad range of learning styles, then try to identify a person's particular learning style so you can aim directly at his or her individual style. If someone is not getting the information, change your approach and present it another way. Use imagery and mnemonics to help your students remember key principles (like safety checks or anchoring fundamentals), and chances are they will retain these key concepts throughout their climbing lifetime.

Lesson Planning

A strategy on how you will present information will help you become a better teacher. The old adage of the "5 Ps" says that "proper preparation prevents poor performance." A simple lesson plan will help you facilitate any lesson you'd like to present.

Venue

Find a crag appropriate for the activity. Is there an alternative site if someone else is using your first choice?

Time

How long will the lesson take? Break down activities into time slots for good time management, giving an appropriate amount of time for each topic.

Materials

Collect and organize the necessary climbing equipment for the lesson. Visual aids and handouts may be beneficial.

Objectives

Set goals for the class or session. For example: "Learning the basic toprope climbing fundamentals, including knots, belaying, safety checks, climbing signals, and basic face climbing technique."

Presentation (Tell/Show/Do)

Make an outline of how you will present the various topics, and how much time will be allotted to each topic. This is called sequencing. For a small group of novices, it may go something like this:

1. Introductions
2. Fitting shoes, harnesses, helmets
3. Orientation and safety talk
4. Harness buckling and safety guidelines
5. Tying the figure eight follow-through
6. Belaying demonstration and ground-school belaying practice
7. Climbing signals
8. Climbing technique demo
9. Students climb and belay
10. Debrief/review at end of day

Evaluate

How will you evaluate the students to know they comprehend, understand, and remember the information you've presented? For example, seeing the students perform all the elements of a proper belay, with all the correct signals, is a good goal for a day one toproping class of novices.

Feedback and Analysis

A review of the day with input from the students gives you valuable feedback from their perspective of how they perceived your presentation of the topics. This allows you to improve and modify your approach for the next time. Getting feedback from your students is key to becoming a better instructor.

Learning from Mistakes

In my career as a rock climbing instructor, I've received training and undergone testing and evaluation of my guiding skills. The toughest lessons, but the most memorable ones, came from the mistakes I made and were critiqued on from my mentors and peers. I've also found, in my role as an examiner for the AMGA Single Pitch Instructor exam, that candidates learn more and remember best from their mistakes when it really counts, when they're being scored in a pass or fail test situation. The harshest lessons in life are the ones we don't soon forget.

With students who have some experience under their belt, asking them to perform a task can tell you where to begin as an instructor. For example, one quick test I give new clients is to simply hand them the end of the rope with the instructions: "Go ahead and tie into the rope." How they accomplish this easy task tells me more about where they're at than even a brief interview.

One method I've used over the years when teaching anchoring fundamentals to a group class in a ground-school setting is to present a concept with a verbal presentation, a demonstration, and then a hands-on practice (tell-show-do). I give each of the students a scenario (e.g., this is the edge, here are the crack systems you can work with, build your anchor system so that your master point is here, etc.), then I let the students build an anchor system to their satisfaction, without constant coaching by me along every step in the process. By letting them finish without my input, they are likely to make some mistakes. Then, as a group, we go around and critique each anchor system setup. In this way everyone learns from everyone's mistakes. The big plus is that it gives me, as an instructor, valuable and instant feedback on whether or not the students have grasped the concepts I've just presented, and shows me what they (or we) need to work on to achieve our objective (e.g., a RENE principle anchor system).

I also use this methodology when teaching a private lesson to one or two students who have some modicum of anchoring experience but have asked for a refresher course. I start by giving them a specific scenario, like rigging a toprope anchor, and let them rig it without any coaching. What I see in the final product of their anchor system helps me decide if they need to start with more basic concepts, or simply move on and build from a solid foundation to more advanced topics. I can then mentally prepare a lesson plan specifically targeted at their skill level and build upon their current foundation to reach our objective for the day.

Teachable Moments

A less formal way to present information is to explain and describe the technique as it comes up during the course of the outing or class. These are what I call teachable moments. For example, when setting up a climbing situation for novices, you can explain to them as they are tying in to the rope the importance of closing the system by tying a stopper knot in the other end of the rope. If they are on a slab climb and their heels come up and they tighten their leg muscles, explaining the correct technique of relaxing the calf muscles and dropping the heels down is a teachable moment. Try to keep it positive. Many teachable moments occur when a simple mistake has been made, and addressing it at that very moment is a great way to teach someone the correct way to do something—the trick is to do it in a positive way that encourages the student to try something new and instantly improve or react positively to a potentially negative situation. Often, the ideal time to address a question is at the moment a particular event that illustrates a key point is occurring. This adds valuable context to the concept.

Taking Kids Climbing

Many kids are natural climbers with an instinctive curiosity and tendency to want to climb things. If you take kids to a rock climbing environment, they'll spontaneously want to explore, climb boulders, and scramble around on the rocks. The obvious danger, however, is that in a fall or slip they can get seriously scraped up, or worse.

Toproping is the safest method to use to take kids climbing. Climbing develops muscular strength, balance, and kinesthetic awareness, and introduces kids to valuable concepts like problem solving, teamwork, and the success that comes from perseverance and determination.

By age eight, nine, or ten, most kids will have reached the level of physical and emotional development to allow them to enjoyably experience climbing in a toprope setting. For younger children, the problem is not with the actual climbing, but having the balance and coordination to successfully be lowered down the climb, as this involves leaning back and weighting the harness, having control over the stance with the legs, and having the proper balance to control body position on the way down. Most very young children (under age five) simply have not yet reached the level of physical coordination required to do this. But I have seen, over the years, cases of precocious children with great balance (as young as age three) who were physically talented enough to climb and be lowered down on a toprope.

Introducing kids to the climbing equipment before they climb helps instill confidence in the equipment. Give them a carabiner and explain how strong it is. Teach them a figure eight knot. Show them how a belay device works. This will assuage their natural fears and help them trust the gear. Demonstrate proper use of their feet on edges and smears, and how to grab different handholds. Kids have a tendency to look up as they climb, rather than look down and watch where they place their feet. Emphasizing to look down and watch their foot all the way to placement on the hold will help.

Set up a short, easy climb on either a low-angle slab or a short wall with abundant hand- and footholds. Teach them the basic climbing signals. For their first time have them climb up a short distance (say 10 feet above the ground), then go through the signals and have them lean back and weight the rope, get into the lowering position, and get lowered back down to the ground. This will show you if they possess the requisite balance to successfully be lowered down the climb. If so, they are ready to climb a bit higher and repeat the same sequence. Take on a climb in small increments, and don't allow them to climb too high above the ground if they're not ready for it. You want the experience to be fun, not terrifying. If they're not yet able to be

Climbing involves teamwork, problem solving, and self-reliance. For young children, always use an adult backup belayer.

lowered down, they can swing around on the rope and play on the rock a little bit. There will be a next time. Just familiarizing them with the rope, harness, and equipment is a good start.

In recent years kids' climbing equipment, including harnesses and helmets for kids, have been introduced to the market. Wearing a helmet

is important, since most young children have not yet developed a kinesthetic awareness of how to fall and stay in control, and are more likely to spin around and bump their head in the event of a fall. Consider a full body harness with straps over the shoulders for small children (under about seventy-five pounds) and very slender kids, as they lack hip bones and could possibly slide out of a harness if they were to fall upside down. One of the most important pieces of equipment for kids are shoes. I've seen many instances where a parent takes a kid climbing, demonstrates the climb (with climbing shoes), then puts the kid on the same climb wearing tennis shoes. This sets the child up for a lesson in frustration, as his or her feet slide off every hold. If you don't want to buy an ever-increasing size range of expensive climbing shoes, an alternative is to buy a resole kit and resole a pair of your child's tennis shoes with climbing rubber. The Five Ten company offers a do-it-yourself resole kit for around $30 (www.fiveten.com).

Teaching Climbing Movement

Just because you can run 100 meters in 9.7 seconds doesn't necessarily mean you'll be a great track and field coach, but it helps. If you have great talent and are able to effectively communicate, you have a winning combination. But I've seen many world-class climbers who were poor teachers, and many competent but not exceptional climbers who were excellent teachers. What I always look for in my climbing school are instructors who have both traits: talented climbers and patient teachers. Climbers who have mastered all the various climbing techniques at a high level can ultimately be the best teachers, as their mechanics and fundamentals are so sound that they have the innate ability to easily demonstrate key concepts. But they also must be effective communicators and have enthusiasm, patience, empathy, and a desire to share their knowledge in a way that truly benefits their students.

When teaching technique I try to present it in a way that most broadly targets the three learning styles: tell, show, and do. First I verbally explain the key elements of a particular technique and what to focus on. Then I demonstrate the technique, climbing the route and describing what I'm doing as I

climb it. If I'm working with another instructor, in a group class situation, I'll have the other instructor belay me while I climb and demonstrate, so the students can watch and listen without having to think about belaying. If I'm the only instructor, I'll have a student belay me, with another student as a backup belayer. If I have only one novice student with limited belaying skills, and I want to demo a climb to illustrate technique, I can either self-belay with an ABD or have the student belay me with an ABD. When I get to the anchor, I can either lower myself (by asking for some slack and clipping a rappel device or ABD on the single strand of rope that goes back down to my belayer) or simply clip into the anchor, go off belay, set up a rappel, and rappel down. If a student belayer is lowering me, before I lean back and let the belayer take my weight, I girth-hitch a sling to the belay loop of my harness and clip it into the single strand of rope running back down to my belayer with a carabiner, so the rope is within my grasp and I can maintain control if for some reason the belayer doesn't.

Before my students start a climb, I try to motivate them and, if necessary, allay their fears: "I know you can do it! Just try to stay as relaxed as you can, and remember, we've got you on a good belay."

I also give them a few specific things to focus on, but not so much that they are overwhelmed: "It's about using the least amount of strength, not the most." Or "Focus on your footwork; watch your foot go right to the hold. Be precise with your footwork. Climb with your eyes, and try to read the rock. When you get to a spot where you feel comfortable, stop for a minute and take a few deep breaths and relax. Remember—we'll keep you tight on the belay, so you can focus on doing the climb."

Once students are climbing, I give them verbal cues to maintain their focus: "Relax. Take a few deep breaths." Or "Keep your heels down." Keep your coaching positive, and encourage them with specific feedback that reinforces good technique: "Nice high step, I like the way you shifted your weight over the left foot." Or "Nice footwork, I like the way you are watching your feet all the way to the holds and placing your feet precisely."

After students finish their climb, I'll give them feedback that includes something specific to reinforce good technique: "Well done, nice footwork, you were really climbing with your eyes and picking out good footholds." Rather than criticize someone for what they did wrong, a better approach is to give them specific tips on what they need to do on the next climb to improve: "Try to relax your ankles and drop your heels down more."

Face climbing comes relatively naturally for most people. Many climbers have indoor climbing gym experience before they venture outside on real rock, so climbing a vertical face with positive holds is usually their forte, as it translates well to gym climbing. The subtleties of delicate friction and smearing are not something you can really learn in a gym, and crack climbing is a whole different animal. Many climbers with extensive gym experience can climb at a 5.11 level indoors, but don't yet have the skills to jam a 5.8 crack. Crack climbing has a tougher learning curve, and it's important to put newcomers to crack climbing on routes that are easy enough to comfortably practice the various jamming skills. Taping their hands or having them wear crack gloves will give them more confidence to go for painful and possibly skin-ripping jams.

One technique we've used in my climbing school (developed by Erik Kramer-Webb) for advanced crack climbing seminars is to have the instructor on a fixed rope (jumaring with mechanical ascenders) alongside the student as the student is climbing and being belayed by another student on a toprope. The instructor can then give the student very specific coaching and demonstration, even putting a hand in the crack to show the best technique for a particular jam. This coaching method has proven very effective, and I've gotten great feedback from students when I've used this particular teaching technique. With only one student, it is still possible to employ this technique: The instructor belays the toprope with an ABD attached to his belay loop, backing it up with a knot on the brake hand side if he wishes to stop and demonstrate a particular jam.

Teaching Rappelling

To teach a novice rappelling technique, site selection is important. Select a site that has a comfortable, flat area on top without a drastic transition from the horizontal to the vertical. The ideal site would have a high master point for the rappel and belay anchor, a flat "desktop" area that extends at least 10 feet back from the edge of the cliff, and a rounded, gradual edge for a comfortable transition to a wall that is angled slightly less than vertical.

In my climbing school we always belay novices on a separate rope when they are learning to rappel. A good system (taught in the AMGA Single Pitch Instructor Course) anticipates any potential problems that may occur during a rappel, and uses a rigging system that is ready to remedy any problem. The system uses a two-rope method: One rope is the rappel line, the other is the belay line. If the length of the rappel is less than half the rope length, the system can be rigged with a single rope, using one end tied to the belayer. The other end goes to the ground. If the rappel is more than half a rope length, two ropes are required. The rappel rope is attached to the anchor with a Munter/mule combination, which is releasable under tension. The rappeller is tied into the belay rope and belayed on a direct belay with a Munter hitch off the anchor.

Let's say the rappeller gets something caught (like long hair, or a shirt) in their rappel device, and can't continue. To fix the problem, you would do the following:

1. Tie off the Munter on the belay line with a mule knot and overhand backup.
2. Release the mule knot on the rappel line and give the rappeller some slack.

Student practicing use of the autoblock on an instructor-belayed rappel, Joshua Tree, California.

Detail of belayed rappel setup. The student is rappelling on the rope in the foreground, tied to the master point with a Munter/mule combination, which is releasable under tension. The instructor is belaying with the direct belay technique using a Munter hitch from an extended master point, created by basketing a double-length (48-inch) nylon runner through the BHK master point, then tied with an overhand knot for redundancy.

3. Have the rappeller fix the problem (e.g., take the hair out of the device).
4. Re-tie the mule knot with overhand backup.
5. Release the mule knot on the belay line and continue belaying the rappel.

In the AMGA Single Pitch Instructor exam, I use this scenario to test the candidate's mastery of the Munter/mule system.

Another good system to use is to tie off the rappel line (either single or double rope) directly to the anchor with a figure eight loop and belay with an autolocking device like a Grigri. It's important to have the belay rope properly flaked so it will feed out without any tangles. Belay with a direct belay off the anchor with the Grigri. If the same snag situation occurs, do this:

1. Tie a backup knot (overhand knot) on the brake strand of the Grigri.
2. Tie a friction knot (prusik or klemheist) on the climber's belay rope and rig a 3:1 Z system.
3. Untie the overhand backup and raise the climber up a few feet.
4. Have the climber resolve the problem.
5. Take off the friction knot and lower the climber until she's back in rappelling mode, then continue to belay the rappeller.

CHAPTER ELEVEN

Risk Management

Every year the American Alpine Club publishes *Accidents in North American Mountaineering,* detailing all the climbing accidents for the year in a comprehensive analysis. Studying what happened to other climbers can heighten your awareness of what to watch out for to avoid a mishap. John Dill, head of Yosemite's Search and Rescue team, studied the most serious climbing accidents that happened in Yosemite Valley from 1970 to 1990. During that time fifty-one climbers died in accidents, 80 percent of them, Dill estimates, "easily preventable." In his article "Staying Alive," Dill points out that state of mind is the key to safety: "It's impossible to know how many climbers were killed by haste or overconfidence, but many survivors will tell you that they somehow lost their good judgment long enough to get hurt. It's a complex subject and sometimes a touchy one. Nevertheless . . . at least three states of mind frequently contribute to accidents: ignorance, casualness, and distraction."

Proper risk management in the toprope environment involves identifying and assessing hazards, making the right decisions to avoid these hazards, then implementing controls and supervision to minimize the risks.

Rockfall

An example of an environmental hazard is rockfall, which can be naturally occurring (caused by melting ice, wind, etc.) or more likely man-made, caused either by someone pulling off or stepping on a loose hold, or in most cases by a rope being pulled or dragged across the top edge of the cliff. Dropped equipment is also a hazard. Setting up a helmet perimeter zone at the base of the cliff minimizes the danger, as does requiring students to not hang out at the very base of the cliff in the rockfall zone unless they are belaying or climbing. An explanation of the risk is appropriate (i.e., why you need to wear your helmet at the base and while belaying and climbing), as is an explanation of the universal verbal signal for a falling rock or dropped piece of equipment: "ROCK!" Being vigilant is the best strategy, especially when other climbers are directly above or at the top of the cliff.

Cindy McCaffrey toproping steep rock on **West Point Crack** *at the Garden of the Gods, Colorado.*
STEWART M. GREEN

Sign at Mountain Warfare Training Center, Leavitt Meadows, California.

Terrain Hazards

Another environmental hazard is simply the terrain itself. If you're working at the top of the cliff, simply falling off the edge is a hazard, as is any steep and exposed terrain involved in scrambling up to the top. In very exposed situations a simple fixed line can be rigged, to which students can be attached using a sling and a prusik knot. Rig by girth-hitching the sling into the harness (through both points where the rope tie-in goes), then attaching it to a short loop of prusik cord with a locking carabiner. A nylon sling is preferable to a Spectra or Dyneema one since it has some modicum of stretch. Sliding the knot along the fixed line affords security and assures you as an instructor that no one can get off-route onto a steeper or more exposed position.

The base of the cliff can also have terrain hazards. The ideal base for group classes would be perfectly flat, but this is often not the case. Showing students the proper approaches to the climb and belay spots and supervising them is important.

Often the most dangerous aspect of taking a large group climbing in a toprope crag setting is their scrambling around on uneven terrain at the base of the cliff, unroped, where they aren't protected by a toprope. The use of ground anchors is important for the belayers in situations where there are chasms and drop-offs adjacent to the belay stances.

Closing the System

In the toprope environment the rope system should always be closed. This simple protocol will prevent many accidents during lowering and rappelling. If a climber is rappelling and one rope end is too short, she can rappel off the short end, which results in her pulling (rapidly!) the now free short end through the rappel anchor, quickly dispatching her to the ground. Another common accident occurs during lowering. If the belayer has wandered out a bit from the cliff, and the rope is too short, and he's not paying attention to the end of the rope, the rope can travel through the belay device, resulting in a dropped climber. A closed system means that both ends of the rope have a knot in them—either the end is tied into someone's harness, or a stopper knot is tied on a free end. This simple safety habit prevents the end of the rope from ever going through a belay or rappel device. Always close the system.

Safety Checks

As an instructor, you are responsible for the group's safety. A protocol for checking every climber and belayer before every climb should be standard procedure. I start with ABC: Check the ground anchor (if used), check the belayer, then check the climber. A proper safety check should be both visual and verbal. As an instructor you must be close enough to clearly see the harness buckle and rope tie-in. A verbal check is important because it lets the student recognize and learn what to check for. The best method is to have the students themselves go through the checks, with your supervision, to get into the habit of a mandatory safety check before every climb.

Anchor

Check the ground anchor to make sure the belayer is in a line between the direction they will be pulled in the event of a fall and the anchor itself. A good way to attach the belayer to the ground anchor is with a clove hitch to a locking carabiner (the end is tied to the front of the belayer's harness with the standard figure eight follow-through knot).

Belayer

Check the belayer's harness, to make sure it is buckled properly. Check the figure eight follow-through knot, to make sure that it is (1) tied properly, and (2) threaded through the correct tie-in points at the front of the harness. Check the belayer's belay device, to make sure the rope is properly threaded through the device, and lastly, check the belayer's locking carabiner on the belay device, to make sure that it is locked. Check that the belayer is wearing her helmet.

Climber

Check the climber's harness, to make sure it is buckled properly. Check the climber's figure eight follow-through knot, to make sure that it is (1) tied properly, and (2) threaded through the correct tie-in points at the front of the harness. Check to ensure the climber is wearing his helmet.

These safety checks are simple, but you'd be surprised how many times I've caught students making a mistake somewhere along these lines. As an instructor you need to do these checks before every climb. It's that simple. Go through the checks with your students until they learn what to look for, and have the belayer/climber pair go through the checks themselves with your supervision.

If you are new to teaching climbing, you might want to come up with an acronym to help you remember what to look for, such as this one I heard one of my AMGA Single Pitch Instructor students use: CRASH. It went like this:

C carabiner (check the locking carabiners)

R rope (check to make sure the rope is not twisted at the top anchor, and check the knots)

A attitude (check with your climber to make sure he or she is ready or has any questions)

S stuff (check for any extraneous stuff on the climber that he or she should remove)

H helmet and harness

A bit of a stretch, but you get the idea. Another one I've heard is BARCK:

B buckles on the harness

A anchor (check the ground anchor)

R rope

C carabiners locked

K knots

Whatever system you use, know what to check for, and be methodical with your safety checks.

Backup Belayers

The purpose of the backup belayer is simple: In case the primary belayer loses control of the brake, the backup belayer, holding the brake strand side of the rope, holds the rope to prevent a fall, essentially backing up the belayer's brake hand. For first-time belayers it is appropriate for the instructor to be the backup belayer. For intermediate-level students who have demonstrated proficiency in belaying techniques, other students are commonly used for backup belayers. As an instructor, when you demonstrate a climb with a student belayer, adding another student as a backup belayer gives you an added layer of protection.

To properly back up a belay, the backup belayer should stand to the side of the belayer and simply hold the rope with both hands, taking in or feeding out rope as needed, leaving enough slack so that the rope is not being tugged from the belayer's brake hand, or in any way impeding the belayer's ability to manage the belay. If the belayer loses control of the brake hand, the backup belayer essentially takes over the braking role. The critical juncture for the backup belayer is when the climber reaches the anchor and transitions into being lowered. The backup belayer can also help the belayer by managing the free end of the rope, preventing any tangles from reaching the belayer.

Experienced instructors often safely manage two climbs at the same time, engaging six participants simultaneously: two climbers, two belayers, and two backup belayers.

Another backup technique is the use of a "catastrophe knot." This is simply an overhand knot tied on the rope on the brake strand side of the belayer's belay device. As an instructor you can use the catastrophe knot if, for some reason, you need to walk away from your role as a backup belayer momentarily. If the climber falls and the belayer loses control, the overhand knot will jam in the belay device, preventing a catastrophic fall.

Backup belayer in action.

Falling

With a sound toprope anchor, a good belayer, a proper tie-in, and good safety checks, the biggest risks the climber faces during the climb are from falling. If the belayer is attentive, and there is minimal slack in the system, the fall will be short and uneventful. For novices, a demo on how to fall is important, showing them the proper position if a fall does occur: a wide stance with the legs, leaning back to weight the harness, not grabbing onto the rope, extending both arms outward against the rock, not clutching the rock or grabbing handholds.

The falls to guard against and watch out for are falls when the climber is too far to the right or left in relationship to the toprope anchor, which result in a swing or pendulum across the rock face;

A discussion and demonstration on proper falling technique is appropriate for novices—feet wide, hanging in the harness, arms outstretched to brace against the rock, not grabbing the rope.

and falls when there is too much slack in the rope. Remember, if using a dynamic rope with a lot of rope in the system, rope stretch can be substantial (dynamic ropes stretch approximately 10 percent even in a toprope fall). When a climber is directly above the ground or a ledge, take particular care to ensure the rope is slightly under tension (especially if you are using a dynamic rope), to guard against rope stretch in the event of a fall.

A directional can be used to prevent a swing in the event of a fall. A directional is a separate piece of gear placed below and to the right or left of the main anchor. For example, if the start of the route is 20 feet to the right of the toprope anchor, and the climber falls near the bottom, she will swing 20 feet to the left during the fall (or even hit the ground). A solid piece placed directly in line above the start would be a directional, preventing the swing. When the climber reaches the piece, she simply unclips and continues to the top. As the climber is being lowered, she re-clips into the directional so that the climb is ready for the next climber.

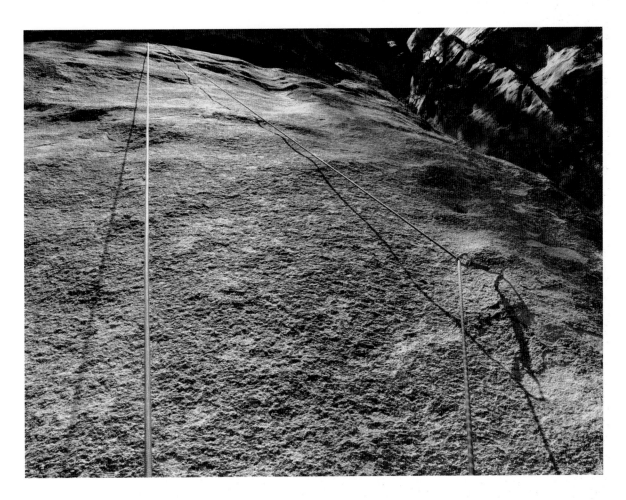

The right side of this toprope setup is clipped into a bolt that will act as a directional to prevent a falling climber from swinging.

CHAPTER TWELVE

Leave No Trace Ethics

You can practice Leave No Trace principles from the moment you step out of your car. The following simple steps will help keep the climbing sites we all share as clean as possible, with minimal degradation to the climbing area and the surrounding environment:

- At popular climbing areas, use the outhouses located at most parking areas before you embark on your approach to that day's chosen cliff.

- Always use marked climber's access trails where they are available. If there is no marked trail to the cliff, minimize your impact by walking on durable surfaces (e.g., a sandy wash, rock slab, or barren ground).

- At popular, easy-access crags, avoid making a beeline from the parking lot straight to the crag without first looking for an established path or trail. Walking off-trail can significantly impact vegetation and cause soil erosion if enough people do it over a period of time.

- If traveling in a group in more remote, pristine areas where no trail exists, fan out instead of walking in single file and try to walk on the most durable surfaces, avoiding fragile vegetation. Don't leave rock cairns to mark the path, as this takes away the challenge of routefinding from

those who prefer to experience it on their own terms.

- If nature calls and you're far from any outhouse, deposit solid human waste well away from the base of any climbing site or wash by digging a cathole 4 to 6 inches deep. Cover and disguise the cathole when you're done. Pack out all toilet paper and tampons in a ziplock bag. Urinate on bare ground or rock, not plants. Urine contains salt, and animals will dig into plants to get at it.

- Leave no trace means just that—pack out everything you bring in, including all trash and food waste (that means apple cores and orange peels, too). Set an example for your group by picking up any trash you find; plan ahead and always carry a trash bag with you when you go out to the crag.

- Don't monopolize popular routes by setting up a toprope and then leaving your rope hanging on the climb, unused. If your climb begins from a campsite, ask permission to climb from the campers if the site is occupied. Minimize your use of chalk, and if you're working a route, clean off any tic marks with a soft brush after you're done. Protect everyone's access to a climbing area by being courteous, beginning with parking only

Patrick Paul belays Mike Roberts at the Needles, California.
GREG EPPERSON

in designated areas and carpooling whenever possible. Noise pollution can be a problem, from blasting tunes on a boom box to yelling and screaming while attempting a hard climb. Be considerate and aware of those around you, and limit your noise production to a reasonable level.

- Pick up all food crumbs and don't feed any wild critters—this habituates them to human food and encourages them to beg and scavenge, sometimes even chewing holes in backpacks to get at food. Consider leaving your dog at home—dogs dig and root up vegetation and stress native wildlife in rural areas. If you do bring your dog, be sure to remove any dog poop from the base of the cliff and the approach trail.

- Leave all natural and cultural objects so that they can be experienced by everyone in their natural setting. If you are climbing in a national forest or national park, obey all regulations concerning the gathering of firewood and other objects.

For more information on Leave No Trace ethics, visit www.lnt.org.

Glossary

ABD (assisted braking device): A device that locks off the rope when a load is quickly applied. The most commonly used ABD is the Petzl Grigri.

aid: means of getting up a climb using other than natural rock features such as handholds, footholds, and cracks, usually by hanging on the rope or equipment to rest and make progress up the climb

aid climbing: using equipment for direct assistance, which allows passage over rock otherwise impossible using free climbing techniques

aid route: a route that can only be ascended using aid climbing techniques

alcove: a cavelike formation or depression in the rock

AMGA (American Mountain Guides Association): a national organization that trains and certifies professional climbing guides and instructors, promotes safety in guiding, and accredits guide services

Aliens: brand name for one type of spring-loaded camming device (SLCD)

American Triangle: a rigging method whereby a sling or cord is threaded through two anchor points and tied in such a manner as to create a triangular configuration that unnecessarily increases the forces on the anchor points. The larger the angle at the base of the triangle, the greater the force on the two anchor points.

arête: a narrow ridge or an outside edge or corner of rock

arm bar: a technique for climbing an off-width crack by inserting an arm into the crack and utilizing counterpressure between the palm on one side of the crack against the triceps

ATC (Air Traffic Controller): a belay/rappel device made by Black Diamond Equipment

backpacker coil: a method of coiling a rope, also known as the "butterfly coil," that reduces kinking in the rope during coiling and facilitates carrying the rope like a backpack

bartack: a high-strength stitch pattern used by climbing equipment manufacturers to sew slings and webbing into loops

backstep: placing the outside edge of the foot on a hold and turning the hip into the rock

bail: to descend or retreat without successfully completing a climb

bashie: a piece of malleable metal that has been hammered into a rock seam as an anchor; used in extreme aid climbing

belay: procedure of protecting a climber by the use of a rope

belay device: a piece of equipment into which the rope is threaded/attached to provide friction for belaying or rappelling

belayer: the person managing the rope on the end opposite the climber; responsible for holding the climber in the event of a fall

belay loop: a sewn loop on the front of the climbing harness to which a rappel or belay device is attached with a locking carabiner; used when belaying and rappelling

beta: prior information about a climb, including sequence, rests, gear, clips, etc. "Running beta" is when someone instructs the climber on how to do the moves as they climb.

beta flash: leading a climb without falling or dogging, but with previous knowledge on how to do the crux moves, such as seeing someone else do the climb

BHK: short for "big honking knot," a double overhand on a bight forming two redundant loops; commonly used as a master point knot on a toprope setup using an extension rope

bight: a bend in the rope where the two strands do not cross; used for knot tying, threading into a belay device, etc.

big wall: a long climb traditionally requiring at least one bivouac, but which may take just a few hours for ace climbers; *see wall*

biner, biners: *see carabiner*

bivi: *see bivouac*

bivouac: to spend the night on a route, usually planned for on a big wall climb; also called bivi

bolt: an artificial anchor placed in a hole drilled for that purpose

bomber: absolutely fail-safe (as in a very solid anchor or big, big handhold); sometimes called bombproof

bombproof: *see bomber*

bong: an almost extinct species of extra-wide pitons, which today have been mostly replaced by large chocks or camming devices

bouldering: short climbs on small boulders or cliffs performed without a belay rope, usually utilizing a small "crash pad" to fall onto and a "spotter" for safety. Climbers do "boulder problems," where the solution is deciphering and executing a series of moves to complete the problem.

bridging: *see stemming*

bucket: a handhold large enough to fully latch onto, like the handle of a bucket; also called a "jug"

buttress: an outside edge of rock that's much broader than an arête

cam: short for spring-loaded camming device; also refers to the single lobe or cam or camming device; also a verb used to describe the act of counterforce wherein a downward and outward force is created against the walls of a crack

Camalot: brand name for one type of spring-loaded camming device (SLCD) manufactured by Black Diamond Equipment. The Camalot was the first SLCD with two axles, which affords a greater range of placement for a given size.

camming device: common term for a spring-loaded camming device (SLCD)

campus: to climb an overhanging section of rock using the arms only; a method of training grip, contact, and upper body strength

carabiner: a high-strength aluminum alloy ring equipped with a spring-loaded snap gate; sometimes called biners

CE: Certified for Europe

ceiling: a section of rock that extends out above your head; an overhang of sufficient size to loom overhead; sometimes called roof

chalk: carbonate of magnesium powder carried in a small "chalk bag," used to prevent fingers and hands from sweating and to provide a firmer grip in warm conditions

chalk bag: a small bag filled with chalk and carried on a belt around a climber's waist

chickenhead: a bulbous knob of rock

chimney: a crack of sufficient size to accept an entire body

chock: *see nut*

chockstone: a rock lodged in a crack

choss, chossy: dirty, loose, rotten, and otherwise unappealing rock

Class 1: mountain travel classification for walking on relatively flat ground and trail hiking

Class 2: mountain travel classification for hiking over rough ground, such as scree and talus; may include the use of hands for stability

Class 3: mountain travel classification for scrambling that requires the use of hands and careful foot placement

Class 4: mountain travel classification for scrambling over steep and exposed terrain; a rope may be used for safety on exposed areas

Class 5: mountain travel classification for technical "free" climbing where terrain is steep and exposed, requiring the use of ropes, protection hardware, and related techniques; *see Yosemite Decimal System (YDS)*

Class 6: mountain travel classification for aid climbing where climbing equipment is used for balance, rest, or progress; denoted with a capital A followed by numerals 0 to 5 (e.g., 5.9/A3 means the free climbing difficulties are up to 5.9 with an aid section of A3 difficulty)

clean: routes that are mostly free of vegetation or loose rock, or where you don't need to place pitons; also the act of removing chocks and other gear from a pitch

clean climbing: climbing that requires only removable protection, no pitons necessary

cleaning tool: a metal pick used to poke and pry nuts from a crack; also known as a "nut tool"

cliff: a high, steep, or overhanging face of rock

clove hitch: a secure and adjustable hitch used to attach a rope to a carabiner

cold shuts: metal hooks commonly found in pairs as anchors atop short sport climbs to facilitate lowering off; can be open, with gates, or welded shut

cordelette: a short length of cord, normally 18 to 25 feet in length, often tied into a loop, used to equalize multiple anchor points. For nylon cord, 7 mm is the standard diameter. High-strength (Technora or Spectra) cord is often used in 5 mm or 6 mm diameter.

crack: a fissure in the rock varying from extremely thin and narrow to as wide as a chimney

crag: another name for a cliff or rock formation

crash pad: a portable foam pad used in bouldering

crimp: a hand grip where the first knuckle is extended and the second knuckle is flexed, allowing the fingertips to rest on a small ledge

crimps: small but positive sharp edges

crux: the most difficult move or sequence of moves on a climb, typically marked on topos with the difficulty rating

dihedral: an inside corner of the climbing surface, formed by two planes of rock, like the angle formed by the pages of an open book; also called an "open book"

direct belay: to belay directly off the anchor

downclimb: a descent without rope, usually when rappelling is unsafe or impractical

drag: the resistance of the rope running through carabiners, commonly referred to as "rope drag"

dynamic rope: a climbing rope with built-in stretch to absorb the energy of a fall, typically around 9 percent stretch under body weight and up to 30 percent in a big fall

dyno: a dynamic move or explosive leap for a hold otherwise out of reach

edge: a small hold, or the act of standing on an edge

edging: using the very edge of the shoe on any clear-cut hold

EN: European Norm

equalette: an anchor-rigging technique using a cordelette, tied by forming a U shape with the cordelette, then tying two overhand knots at the center point, about 12 inches apart. A carabiner is clipped into each loop of cord between the knots to create a self-equalizing rig with minimal extension. The four strands, or "arms," of the cordelette can be attached to various anchors.

exposure: a relative situation where a climb has particularly noticeable sheerness

extension: the potential for an anchor system's slings or cord to lengthen if one piece in the anchor system fails, causing a higher force on the remaining anchor or anchors

fall factor: an equation that calculates the severity of a fall: the total distance of the fall divided by the length of rope from the belay

finger crack: a crack climbed by wedging and jamming the fingers into the crack

finger jams: wedging the fingers into constrictions in a crack

fireman's belay: a technique used to belay a rappelling climber by pulling down on the rope below the rappeller, creating tension that stops the rappeller from further movement down the rope

first free ascent: the first free climb of a route previously climbed by aid climbing

fist jam: placing and wedging a fist sideways in a crack with the fingers curled inward toward the palm, providing a secure enough jam to pull on

fixed anchor: any permanent anchor left for all climbers to utilize, typically bolts or pitons

flag: a climbing technique using a limb as a counterbalance

flakes: a wafer or section of rock where a crack runs parallel to the plane of the main rock structure, as opposed to a "straight-in" crack that runs perpendicular to the plane of the main rock face

flaking a rope: uncoiling a rope into a loose pile, with one end on the bottom and the other end on the top of the pile; also called "stacking" a rope

flared crack: any crack that increases in dimension either inward or outward

flash: free climbing a route from bottom to top on your first try, without falling or hanging on the rope

footwork: the art and method of standing on holds

Fox System: a toprope rigging technique using an extension rope to create both a tether and an extended master point

free: *see free climb*

free ascent: *see free climb*

free climb: the upward progress gained by a climber's own efforts, using hands, feet, and any part of the body on available features, unaided or free of attending ropes and gear. Rope is only used to safeguard against injury, not for upward progress or resting. Opposite of aid climb; also called free or free ascent.

free solo: free climbing a route without the use of a rope

friction hitch: one of several hitches tied around a rope using a piece of smaller cord or a sling, which grips when weight is applied, but can be loosened and slid up the rope when not under tension; commonly used to ascend a rope and in self-rescue techniques

Friend: the name of the original spring-loaded camming device (SLCD) designed by Ray Jardine and marketed by the Wild Country Company in 1977. The word *friend* became a generic term for any SLCD.

frog step: bringing one foot up, then the other, while keeping your torso at the same level, forming a crouched or "bullfrog" position

gaston: to grip handholds with the hands in a thumbs-down position, then pull outward, like prying apart elevator doors. Can also be one hand in the thumbs-down position on a handhold above and to the side of the body.

girth-hitch: a hitch used to connect webbing or cord around a feature to create an anchor by looping around the object then back through the sling or cord

gobies: hand abrasions

Grade: a rating that tells how much time an experienced climber will take on a given climb, referring to the level of commitment required by the average climbing team; denoted by Roman numerals

Grade I: a climb that may take only a few hours to complete

Grade II: a climb that may take three to four hours

Grade III: a climb that may take four to six hours, typically done in half a day

Grade IV: a climb that may take a full day

Grade V: a climb that normally takes two days, requiring a bivouac

Grade VI: a climb that normally takes two or more days on the wall, requiring several bivouacs by the average party

Grigri: a belay device with assisted braking manufactured by Petzl

gripped: extremely scared

ground anchor: an anchor used to secure a belayer at the base of a climb

hangdog, hangdogging: hanging on the rope to rest; not a free ascent. Sport climbers will often "hangdog" up a route to practice the moves and prepare for a later "free" ascent.

headwall: a much steeper section of cliff, found toward the top

heel hooking: hooking the heel on a large hold on overhanging rock above your head and pulling with the leg much like a third arm

hex, hexes: *see hexentric*

hexentric: a six-sided chock made by Black Diamond Equipment that can be wedged into cracks; commonly called a hex

highball: a term used to describe bouldering problem that is high off the ground

hip belay: to belay by wrapping the rope around your waist to create friction

horn: a generally small, knoblike projection of rock

indirect belay: to belay from the harness, not directly off the anchor

jam: wedging feet, hands, fingers, or other body parts to gain purchase in a crack

Joshua Tree System: a rigging technique for toproping using an extension rope and a V configuration to create a master point over the edge of the cliff

jug: a handhold shaped like a jug handle

jumar: term commonly used to refer to a device used to ascend a climbing rope; also a verb, i.e., "jumaring" the rope means ascending the rope

killer: extraordinarily good

latch: to successfully grip a hold

layback: climbing maneuver that entails pulling with the hands while pushing with the feet; also called lieback

laybacking: *see layback*

lead: to be the first on a climb, belayed from below, and placing protection to safeguard a fall

lieback: climbing maneuver that entails pulling with the hands while pushing with the feet; also called layback

liebacking: *see lieback*

line: the path of the route, usually the line of least resistance between other major features of the rock

lock-off: hanging by one arm on a single handhold with enough strength to allow the other hand to release its grip and move up to a new handhold

loop strength: the minimum breaking strength of a sling or cord when tested in a single, continous loop; like a Dyneema sewn into a loop with bartacked stitching, or cord tied into a loop with a knot

lunge: an out-of-control dynamic move, a jump for a far-off hold

magic X: *see sliding X*

manky: of poor quality, as in "a manky finger jam" or "manky protection placement"

mantle: a series of climbing moves enabling you to grab a feature (like a ledge) and maneuver up to where you're standing on it, usually accomplished by pulling up, then pressing down with one or both palms while bringing up one foot (similar to getting out of the deep end of a swimming pool)

mantleshelf: a rock feature, typically a ledge with scant holds directly above

mantling: the act of surmounting a mantleshelf

master point (aka power point): the equalized point in an anchor system; the point a climber clips into

micro-nut: a very small nut used mainly for aid climbing

mountaineering: reaching mountaintops using a combination of skills (such as rock climbing and ice climbing), usually involving varying degrees of objective hazards

move: one of a series of motions necessary to gain climbing distance

multipitch: a route with multiple belay stations (rope lengths)

Munter hitch: a hitch used for belaying that requires no gear other than a carabiner

natural anchor: an anchor made from a feature occurring in nature, such as a chockstone, rock tunnel, horn, tree, boulder, etc.

nut: a wedged-shaped piece of metal designed to be used as an anchor in a crack; also called a chock

nut tool: a metal pick used to tap and pry nuts to facilitate removal or "cleaning"

off-width: a crack that is too wide to use as a finger, hand, or fist jam but too narrow to get inside and climb as a chimney

on-sight: to successfully climb a route without prior knowledge or experience of the moves

opposition: nuts, anchors, or climbing maneuvers that are held in place by the simultaneous stress of two forces working against each other

overhang, overhanging: a section of rock that is steeper than vertical

peg: *see piton*

pinch grip: a handhold where the thumb pinches in opposition to the fingers on either side of a projection

pinkpoint: to lead (without falling) a climb that has been pre-protected with gear and rigged with quickdraws

pins: *see pitons*

pin scar: a mark of damage left in a crack by repeated placement and removal of pitons

pitch: the distance between belays

pitons: metal spikes of various shapes that are hammered into the rock to provide anchors in cracks; sometimes called pins or pegs. These types of anchors were common up to the 1970s, but are rarely used today.

power point: *see master point*

pre-equalized: tying off an anchor system for an anticipated force in only one direction

pro: *see protection*

protection: the anchors used to safeguard the leader; sometimes called pro. Until the 1970s, protection devices were almost exclusively pitons—steel spikes that were hammered into cracks in the rock. Since then, various nuts and camming devices have virtually replaced pitons as protection devices. These chocks and cams are fitted into cracks, and the rope is attached to them. In the absence of cracks, permanent bolt anchors are installed into the rock. The leader clips into the protection and proceeds to climb past it. If the leader falls, he or she will travel at least twice the distance from above the last point of protection (rope stretch adds more distance).

prusik: both the knot and any means by which you mechanically ascend a rope

quad: a rigging technique accomplished by doubling a cordelette and clipping it to two anchor points, quadrupling the strands. Two overhand knots are tied in the four strands, and carabiners are clipped to three of the four strands between the knots, creating a self-equalizing anchor system with minimal extension.

quickdraws: short slings with carabiners at both ends that help provide drag-free rope management for the leader

quick link: an aluminum or steel screw link often found on rappel anchors, mostly bought from hardware stores, although some manufacturers make CE certified quick links for climbing (like the Petzl maillon rapide)

rack: the collection of gear a climber takes up the climb

rappel: to descend by sliding down a rope, typically utilizing a mechanical braking device

rapping: informal term for rappelling

redpoint: to lead a route from bottom to top in one push, clipping protection as you go, without falling or resting on protection

redirected belay: to belay by running the rope through a belay device attached to the harness, then back through an anchor

RENE: acronym for Redundancy, Equalization, and No Extension

Rocks: brand name for a line of passive nuts developed by Mark Valance and sold by Wild Country

roof: a section of rock that extends out above your head; sometimes called a ceiling

rope direct belay: to belay from an extended master point using the climbing rope

R-rated climbs: protection or danger rating for climbs with serious injury potential; protection may be sparse or "runout," or some placements may not hold a fall

runner: *see sling*

runout: the distance between two points of protection; often refers to a long stretch of climbing without protection

sandbagging: the "shameful" practice of a first ascent team underrating the actual difficulty of a given route

second: the second person on a rope team, usually the leader's belayer

self-equalizing: an anchor system that adjusts to withstand a force in multiple directions

send it: an emphatic statement to someone encouraging him or her to hang in and finish a route without falling

sharp end: the lead climber's end of the rope

shelf: the pre-equalized point on a cordelette directly above the master point knot; all loops must be clipped for redundancy

shred: to do really well; to dominate

sidepull: pulling on a vertically aligned hold to the side of the body

signals: a set of commands used between climber and belayer

slab: a less than vertical, or low-angle, section of a rock face

SLCD (spring-loaded camming device): *see Friend*

sliding X (aka magic X): a self-equalizing sling rigged between two anchor points

sling: webbing sewn or tied into a loop; also called a runner

smear, smearing: standing on a sloping foothold and utilizing friction in order to adhere to the rock

"soft" ratings: ratings deemed harder than the actual difficulty of a given route

spring-loaded camming device (SLCD): *see Friend*

sport climbing: similar to traditional rock climbing but with protection and anchors (bolts) already in place. Instead of using nuts and cams, the climber uses quickdraws, clipping bolts for protection. Most sport climbing is face climbing and is usually only one pitch in length, but can be multipitch. With the danger element removed, the emphasis is on technique and doing hard moves.

spotter: a person designated to slow the fall of a boulderer, especially to keep the boulderer's head from hitting the ground

stance: a standing rest spot, often the site of a belay

static rope: a rope with virtually no stretch

stem, stemming: the process of counterpressuring with the feet between two widely spaced holds; sometimes called bridging

stopper knot: a safety knot tied on the end of a rope to prevent accidents

Stoppers: brand name for one of the original (and now one of the most commonly used) wedge-shaped tapered nut deigns, sold by Black Diamond Equipment

sustained: climbing adjective that indicates the continuous nature of the climb

tail: the length of the end of a rope protruding from a knot

TCU (three-cam unit): a type of spring-loaded camming device (SLCD) with just three cams instead of four

tensile strength: the minimum breaking strength of a sling, cord, or rope when tested on a single strand

thin: a climb or hold of relatively featureless character

thread: a sling or cord looped through a tunnel in the rock structure

topo: a detailed diagram showing a climbing route up a cliff

toprope: a belay from an anchor point above that protects the climber from falling even a short distance

toproping: *see toprope*

trad: *see traditional rock climbing*

traditional rock climbing: climbing a route where the leader places gear (nuts and cams) for protection and anchors, to be removed later by the second or "follower"; as opposed to sport climbing, which relies solely on bolts for protection and anchors; also called trad climbing

traverse: to move sideways, without altitude gain

Tricam: a mechanical wedge that acts both as a nut and as a cam

tweak: to injure, as in "a tweaked finger tendon"

UIAA: Union Internationale des Associations d'Alpinisme

undercling: grabbing a hold (usually a flake) with the palm up and fingers underneath the hold, then pulling outward with the arm while pushing against the rock with the feet, much like a lieback

V system: the universal bouldering language, established in the early 1990s at Hueco Tanks, Texas. Ratings range from V0 to V16, with V0 being the easiest and V15 being roughly equivalent to 5.15b YDS.

vector: a measurement of force and direction in anchor systems

wall: a long climb traditionally done over multiple days, but which may take just a few hours for ace climbers; *see big wall*

water knot: a knot used to tie a loop of webbing

webbing: synthetic fiber woven flat like a strap, used to make slings. Nylon webbing was used exclusively for slings up to the 1990s; now slings are also made from Spectra and Dyneema webbing.

wired: known well, as in "a wired route"

work, worked, or working: to practice the moves of a difficult route via toprope or hangdogging

X-rated climbs: protection or danger rating for climbs with groundfall and death potential

YDS: *see Yosemite Decimal System*

Yosemite Decimal System (YDS): the American grading scale for identifying technical difficulty of routes, where 5 denotes the class, and the numerals following the decimal point indicate the difficulty rating (5.0 to 5.15), usually according to the most difficult move. Subgrades (a, b, c, and d) are used on climbs rated 5.10 and harder.

Z system: a raising system that uses a 3:1 mechanical advantage

Index

About the Author

Bob Gaines began rock climbing at Joshua Tree in the 1970s. Since then he has pioneered over 400 first ascents in the park. Bob began his career as a professional rock climbing guide in 1983 and is the owner of Vertical Adventures Rock Climbing School, which offers classes and guided climbs at Joshua Tree. In 2008 Vertical Adventures was voted the #1 rock climbing school in America by *Outside* magazine.

Bob has worked extensively in the film business as a climbing stunt coordinator. He has coordinated over thirty television commercials, and he was Sylvester Stallone's climbing instructor for the movie *Cliffhanger.* Bob doubled for William Shatner in the movie *Star Trek V,* as Captain Kirk free soloing on El Capitan in Yosemite.

An AMGA Certified Rock Climbing Instructor, Bob currently teaches the AMGA Single Pitch Instructor Course at Joshua Tree. He has worked extensively training US military special forces, including US Navy Seal Team 6, and is known for his technical expertise in anchoring and rescue techniques.

Bob is also the author of *Best Climbs Joshua Tree National Park,* and the co-author of *Rock Climbing Tahquitz and Suicide Rocks* (with Randy Vogel) and *Climbing Anchors* (with John Long). Bob splits his time between his residences in Irvine and Joshua Tree, California.

Photo by Patty Kline

PROTECTING CLIMBING **ACCESS** SINCE 1991

ACCESS FUND

| JOIN US |
WWW.ACCESSFUND.ORG